BREAKING THROUGH:

Creating Opportunities for America's Women and Minority-Owned Businesses

SUSAN PHILLIPS BARI

Copyright © 2013 Susan Phillips Bari and Women's Business Enterprise National Council

Published by the Women's Business Enterprise National Council

Washington, DC

All rights reserved.

ISBN-13: 978-1484073407
ISBN-10: 1484073401

To the WBENC staff, the Corporate members, Regional Partner Organizations and Certified Women-owned Businesses that keep the dream alive.

TABLE OF CONTENTS

Acknowledgements	1
Foreword	3
Preface	5
Introduction	**10**
Where Are We Now? The Status Of Women and Minority-owned Business In America	11
Cheat Sheet: Supplier Diversity Classifications	13
About the Case Study WBEs	16
What We Will Cover	20
Chapter One: Big Bucks from Big Business	**23**
Why is There a Need for Supplier Diversity Programs?	24
The Right Stuff	26
What Defines a Corporate Supplier Diversity Program?	27
How Do I Decide Which Corporations to Target?	30
Who Works In the Supplier Diversity Field?	33
A Day In the Life	35
Cheat Sheet: Getting to Know Your Supplier Diversity Contacts	36
Don'ts or WBEs	37
When Do Companies Make Their Purchases From Diverse Suppliers?	38
Where Do I Get Started?	38
Case Study: Cindy Funaro Towers, Esq., JuriSolutions	39
Chapter Two: Becoming Certified	**41**
The History of Certification	41
Want to Be a Million-Dollar Business? Get Certified!	43
The Steps to Certification	43
WOSB Certification	44
Criteria for Certification as a WOSB	45
Off and Running!	53
Case Study: Rebecca Boenigk, CEO & Chairman of the Board, Neutral Posture, LLC.	55
Chapter Three: Catching the Big Fish: Marketing	**59**
The Eleven Commandments of MWBE Marketing	60
Success Story: Julie Rhodes, President & CEO, Kleenslate Concepts	66
Cheat Sheet: Defining Your Value Proposition	73
Cheat Sheet: Sample Press Releases	81

Breaking Through

Cheat Sheet: Speak Up! Making the Most of Your Public Speaking	85
Cheat Sheet: Tips for Preparing for a Media Interview	92
Case Study: Patty Klein, President & CEO, A-Plus Meetings & Incentives	99
Chapter Four – Networking	**104**
Getting to Know You: Associations and Networking Organizations	109
Where to Start?	113
Making the Most of Your Memberships	123
Attending Networking Events	127
Success Story: Jennifer Collins, President & CEO of The Event Planning Group, LLC	130
Networking Nirvana: Supplier Diversity Trade Shows & Buyers Marts	131
Networking Mistakes to Avoid	137
Case Study: Ranjini Poddar, President, Artech Information Systems, LLC	139
Chapter Five – Alternative and Advanced Supplier Strategies	**142**
Stragetic Alliances	144
Cheat Sheet: Forming a Strategic Alliance	145
Second-Tier Opportunities	146
Cheat Sheet: How to Become a Second-Tier Supplier	150
Become a Business Solution Partner	153
Success Story: Billie Bryant, President & CEO, Cesco	154
Matchmaker, Matchmaker, Make Me a Match	155
Cheat Sheet: WBENC MatchMaker Meeting Program Time Line	156
Making the Most of a Matchmaker Meeting	158
Case Study: Camilla Sullivan, Principal, Visionista	162
Chapter Six – The First "P" of Supplier Diversity Success: PREPARATION for the Big Meeting and Beyond	**165**
Update Your Data	166
Find Out Who Makes the Decisions	166
Everything You Need to Know About Technology...But Were Too Busy Checking Your E-mail to Ask	173
Ten Technology Tips	175
Case Study: Janet Crenshaw Smith, CEO, Ivy Planning Group, LLC	188

Chapter Seven – The Second "P" of Supplier Diversity Success: Planning and Presenting your PITCH	***192***
Presentation Content	192
Cheat Sheet: What the Buyer Wants to Know	196
Cheat Sheet: Tips for a Perfectly Presentable Presentation	203
Pitch Meeting Dos and Don'ts	206
After the Meeting	213
Case Study: Cathi Coan, CEO Techway Services	214
Chapter Eight – The Third "P" of Supplier Diversity Success: PERSEVERANCE	***218***
The Waiting Game	220
While You Wait	222
Success Story: Julie Levi, Founder and President, Progressive Promotions, Inc.	227
Case Study: Tara Abraham, Chairman & Co-CEO, Accel inc.	231
Chapter Nine – Keeping the Contracts	***235***
Cheat Sheet: Contract Law 101	236
Best Practices for Keeping Contracts	239
Case Study – Nancy Williams, Co-President, ASAP Solutions	242
Afterword	246
Appendix A: WBENC Regional Partner Organization (RPOs)	249
Appendix B: Useful Abbreviations	264
Appendix C: Resource Guide	266
Appendix D: Examples of a Corporate "What We Purchase"	268

ACKNOWLEDGMENTS

It is trite to say "it takes a village," but writing this book took a community—the Women's Business Enterprise National Council community. We wish to acknowledge the many individuals and organizations that have made this third edition and prior editions of *Breaking Through* possible.

The first and second editions were edited by Ginger Conrad, long-serving publisher of *MBE Magazine* and dedicated member of the WBENC Board of Directors. While she is currently enjoying retirement, her skill and dedication are reflected in these pages.

Lindsey Pollak was my "book coach" when I first got the idea to write *Breaking Through*. She was a recent author herself at the time, and we ran into one another at an Office Depot event. When I mentioned I had always wanted to write a book but never could find the time, she said, "I can help you." Lindsey kept me on deadline and helped me to organize my thoughts and ideas into a coherent book. She has since written a second book *("Getting from College to Career: Your Essential Guide to Succeeding in the Real World*) that has led to her current status as a keynote speaker on college campuses and a consultant to corporations on Generation Y employees.

A very special thank you to Camilla Sullivan, Laura Rehbehn, and their colleagues at Visionista for the design of both the cover and the interior of this third edition. They take an idea and turn it into a visual with remarkable creativity.

I want to thank the many women business owners who have shared their stories and the corporate supplier diversity executives who share their expertise in these pages and daily for their corporations.

To the leadership of WBENC, the members of the Board, Leadership Council, and Women's Enterprise Leadership Forum

Susan Phillips Bari

who promote the book with their constituents, I will be forever grateful.

Most importantly I want to thank WBENC CEO Pamela Prince-Eason for understanding the importance of *Breaking Through* as a resource for the organization and its constituents. Pam made this third edition possible.

FOREWORD

FROM PAMELA PRINCE-EASON, PRESIDENT AND CEO, AND LAURA TAYLOR, CHAIR OF THE BOARD

There is no question that, supplier diversity builds business and strengthens all participants. Since 1997, the Women's Business Enterprise National Council has had the goal of fostering diversity in the world of commerce. We recognized from the outset that it promotes innovation and opens new channels of revenue, and the partnership it creates fuels the economy.

The Women's Business Enterprise National Council is a strong advocate for the role played by women-owned businesses in the corporate and government marketplaces. Our members know firsthand the value that women entrepreneurs bring to the supply chain and to the economy overall.

As we have grown throughout the years, through our programs and partnerships we have developed a platform that unites corporations with thousands of highly skilled companies that meet the rigorous requirements to attain Women Business Enterprise (WBE) certification. And, as of 2011, we began providing certification for the US Small Business Administration's Women-Owned Small Business (WOSB) program, expanding the ability of WBEs to contribute to economic growth in both the public and the private sectors.

Our platform is at the "CORE" of all we do. Let us explain.

Certification (C) is the cornerstone of WBENC's value proposition. The WBENC certification standard is the most relied-upon certification of women-owned businesses by public, private, nonprofit, and government entities and has become the model for the expansion of certification globally.

Opportunities (O) deliver the programming and networking needs of our constituents. WBENC is committed to connecting our corporate members, government members, and WBEs with women's business enterprises in the most effective ways.

Resources (R) are provided throughout our network to address the challenges women face in building and growing a business. 'WBENC provides WBEs the needed and most effective education, support, and tools to grow their businesses effectively and to meet the needs of our corporate and government members.

Engagement (E) of our constituents is a key to success throughout our network. We believe that involvement strengthens our existing relationships and fosters new ones. Recognition that promotes the success of key constituents creates a better awareness of leading practices required to create success for women entrepreneurs and inspires all to reach higher standards of performance.

You will learn more about our CORE throughout this book. We invite you to join forces with WBENC. Our commitment and collaboration drive progress and are playing a significant role in fueling our nation's economy and creating job growth.

Pamela Prince-Eason   *Laura Taylor*

PREFACE

A month before my college graduation in 1967, all seniors were informed we must participate in an exit interview with the guidance department. Every woman student heard the same question: "Do you want to be a teacher or a nurse?" If the answer was neither, the next question was "How many words a minute do you type?" With limited typing skills and no desire to change bedpans, I opted for teaching. My mother and aunts assured me that this was an honorable and rewarding profession that would provide me the flexibility—once I had identified the perfect husband—to be home when my kids returned from school or were on vacation.

I loved teaching and found that it was rewarding as promised. However, after a few years of watching one hundred children go through puberty at 8:00 a.m. every morning, I yearned for more adult interaction. I was also broke and working part-time jobs selling men's haberdashery to make the living wage. I needed to make up for the fact that Mr. Perfect Husband had not yet arrived on the scene.

Eventually, I found a part-time position, after school and on Saturdays, filing and doing other administrative chores for a successful small-business owner who served as a manufacturers' representative for several companies. In addition to the linens and domestics lines of merchandise he carried, there was a "piece goods" line of on-the bolt fabrics.

I asked if he could provide me with some sample fabric, since I made many of my own clothes. He did me one better and offered to pay me to make "model garments" that he could use as part of his sales pitch. ("I have a home sewer named Susan who samples each of these fabric lines before I show them to you," he would say to clients, "and Susan assures me that this fabric is easy to work with and produces a satisfactory result for the home sewer.") He let me keep the garments once the selling season ended. This arrangement worked well for me. At the time I did not even realize I had just launched my first business.

My business initiation went a step further when I was called upon to make the pitch myself to a buyer who was visiting the office one Saturday morning. After the buyer had signed the largest order to date and left, my boss asked if I would consider leaving my teaching position to join his sales team. At nearly double my salary as a teacher, plus the promise of additional commission-based bonuses—and no puberty problems among the buyers I would be calling on—this was an easy decision to make.

I received preliminary training by the manufacturer and then went out on my own to call on buyers for department store chains, mom-and-pop operations, and mass merchandisers. I was ecstatic. Three months later, my balloon burst when the IRS came calling at my boss's door. "Last hired, first fired" (yes, me) was the result. I did not know where I would go to find employment, but I did know it would not be back to the schoolhouse. I had caught the business bug.

After several fruitless job interviews (in the early 1970s there were few women in sales in any field), I decided to see if I could start my own manufacturers' representative business. After three days of visiting each of the exhibiting companies at a trade show, I identified six companies that would let me represent them on a commission basis in New England. One even offered a small advance on commission each month to tide me over until the seasonal sales started translating into post-delivery paychecks.

Now I was really in business. I did not know the word at the time, but I was an *entrepreneur*. I was also the first woman commissioned sales representative in this industry. Amazingly, an industry selling fabric to home sewers—99.9 percent of whom were women—had no women selling its products to stores. It would be many years before I translated this industry-based perspective into an awareness of the inequities existing for all women and all industries, felt even more strongly by women of color.

SELLING TO BIG BUSINESS

My repping experience taught me another lesson that has expanded over the years and played an important role in my participation in the founding of the Women's Business Enterprise National Council (WBENC, pronounced *wee-bank*): It is easier to make a living selling to a mass merchandiser who has three hundred stores than to the mom-and-pop shop on the corner. Bigger contracts are better than smaller contracts. Commissions based on sales to three hundred stores resulting from a meeting with one buyer are more efficient and lucrative than commissions based on sales to three hundred stores resulting from meetings with three hundred buyers.

But, as I quickly learned, it is not easy to get in the door of large corporations to get the bigger contracts. For women and minority-owned firms, this is particularly challenging. I became determined to find my way in.

I first heard about the existence of supplier diversity programs in 1994. They are departments that exist in many large American corporations to create mutually beneficial business relationships between previously disadvantaged women and minority business owners and large corporations that can purchase their products and services. Supplier diversity departments serve as internal advocates for diverse business owners. I quickly determined that these programs represented an enormous opportunity to level the playing field for women entrepreneurs like me. Their existence provides an extraordinary new door to opportunity. However, I soon discovered that too few women and minority-owned firms knew of or took advantage of this marketing opportunity.

At the time, the National Minority Supplier Development Council (NMSDC) had already been founded (in 1972) to vet and certify minority business enterprises and to help minority business owners access the opportunities in the corporate market. But no organization existed to help women grow their businesses through corporate opportunities.

In 1997, with the support of eleven forward-thinking corporations, four women's business organizations, and many dedicated women business owners, we launched the Women's Business Enterprise National Council (WBENC). Our goal was, and still is, to enhance opportunities for women business enterprises in America's major business markets—to help women find the doors to opportunity and break through those doors to achieve enormous growth and success.

WBENC certifies thousands of women-owned businesses each year (verifying that they are at least 51 percent women-owned, operated and controlled) through programs in fourteen regionally based organizations, and then helps connect those certified women-owned businesses with corporate purchasing officers. Now the Small Business Administration's (SBA) Women-Owned Small Business (WOSB) Federal Contract Program will provide greater access to federal contracting opportunities for WOSBs and economically disadvantaged women-owned small businesses (EDWOSBs). The program allows contracting officers, for the first time, to set aside specific contracts for certified WOSBs and EDWOSBs and will help federal agencies achieve the existing statutory goal of 5 percent of federal contracting dollars being awarded to WOSBs

As a new third-party certifier of the SBA's WOSB Federal Contract Program, WBENC has introduced a Women-Owned Small Business Government Certification (WOSBGC) Program.

The WBENC website (www.wbenc.org), Internet database, conferences, and business fairs provide opportunities for major corporations and women-owned businesses to meet and do business with each other. Educational programs—such as the Tuck-WBENC Executive Program, presented with the Amos Tuck School at Dartmouth College and underwritten by IBM for the past decade—provide the tools for women business owners to grow their management skills along with their new contract opportunities. The tips, stories, advice, and insights I collected as WBENC president and as a woman entrepreneur are presented in this book along with new WBE case studies and commentaries from corporate supplier diversity professionals.

I am grateful that I was able to translate my entrepreneurial impulses to social entrepreneurship as the leader for more than ten years of a nonprofit organization dedicated to providing assistance in the form of opportunity to other women entrepreneurs. Now I am back in the for-profit world to pass the leadership baton to other dedicated and passionate women leaders.

Throughout its history, WBENC has grown through the participation of America's largest and most respected companies, who share a commitment to women's business growth. I am grateful to the members of the board, the leaders of the regional partner organizations, and the two presidents who succeeded me to sustain and grow the organization. Through my experience at WBENC, I am now able to help women and minority-owned businesses develop growth strategies based on the marketing insight I developed selling piece goods many years ago. With this book, I can now bring these strategies, tools, and opportunities to an even larger audience: women and minority business owners like you.

Breaking Through: Creating Opportunities for America's Women and Minority-Owned Businesses provides you with an overview of the huge opportunity available through supplier diversity programs, and shares my secrets for marketing your business to Fortune 1000 companies and government agencies and keeping the business you acquire. Selling to these major market places—corporate America and the federal government—is not easy, but it is the key to extraordinary growth for your business and our national economy.

Susan Phillips Bari, President Emeritus

Introduction

Did you know that more than twenty-three million businesses compose the United States business landscape? Yet, of these twenty-three million there are only one thousand companies in the famous Fortune 1000 list of major corporations. We frequently forget that each and every one of those big companies started as a small business and, more importantly, that these large companies need to do business with smaller companies in order to survive and thrive.

The Fortune 1000 started with visionary entrepreneurs who risked their resources and reputations to build corporations that provide each of us with everything from cell phone service to the computers on our desktops and in our hands to the wheels on our luggage to air-conditioning in our offices and cars to the cars themselves. Like most of us who have started companies, these entrepreneurs used personal savings, a mortgage on their homes, or even their personal credit cards to provide the start-up funds necessary to begin operations. Breaking through the barriers in their paths from dreams to great riches and professional recognition required access to capital, the ears of investors, and an open door to purchasing officials who could buy or invest in *their* products. Perhaps most importantly, they required a strong strategy for success.

It is to the latter business need that this book is dedicated: finding the right strategies to open doors, finding supporters, and gaining access to growth opportunities for women and minority business owners. While access to capital is crucial for small-business growth and success, *Breaking Through* focuses on helping small and medium-sized businesses secure contracts with large corporations—the big sales that lead to enormous and lasting growth. But big opportunity does not guarantee big success. You need smart strategies.

How do you, as a small or medium-sized business owner, build a strategy to do business with the Fortune 1000 or the federal government? Here comes the good news: If you are one of over eleven million women or minority business owners in the United States, you have unique opportunities: corporate supplier diversity programs and the new WOSB program, which will be explained in depth shortly. *Breaking Through* offers insider information on these programs and how they can help you grow your business. Beyond information, the following pages provide proven marketing strategies specifically crafted to maximize supplier diversity opportunities for your company. *Breaking Through* is the competitive advantage you need to do business with corporate America.

WHERE ARE WE NOW? THE STATUS OF WOMEN AND MINORITY-OWNED BUSINESS IN AMERICA

Women-owned and led firms are a promising segment of our national economy. According to the third annual *State of Women-Owned Businesses Report,* commissioned by American Express OPEN,

> As of 2013, it is estimated that there are over 8.6 million women-owned businesses in the United States, generating over $1.3 trillion in revenues and employing nearly 7.8 million people.
>
> • Between 1997 and 2013, when the number of businesses in the United States increased by 41%, the number of women-owned firms increased by 59%—a rate 1½ times the national average. Indeed, the growth in the number (up 59%), employment (up 10%) and revenues (up 63%) of women-owned firms over the past 16 years exceeds the growth rates of all but the largest, publicly traded firms—topping the growth rates in number, employment and revenue of all privately held businesses over this period.

- Despite the fact that the number of women-owned firms continues to grow at a rate exceeding the national average, and now accounts for 29% of all enterprises, women-owned firms only employ 6% of the country's workforce and contribute just under 4% of business revenues—roughly the same share they contributed in 1997. When large, publicly traded firms are excluded, women-owned firms comprise 30% of the privately held firm population and contribute 14% of employment and 11% of revenues.

- Combining equally owned firms with women-owned enterprises finds that women-owned and equally owned firms number nearly 13.6 million as of 2013, generate over $2.7 trillion in revenues, and employ nearly 15.9 million people. Together, these firms represent 46% of US firms and contribute 13% of total employment and 8% of firm revenues.

What defines these businesses? They are small, medium, and large; rural, suburban, and urban; product and service based; family owned and global; product and service oriented; traditional, nontraditional, and everything in between. The diversity of women-owned businesses selling to corporate America is truly astounding. This book will share strategies of WBENC-certified businesses ranging from sole proprietorships to multinational corporations.

Minority businesses also are rapidly accessing the American dream through entrepreneurship. Did you know that Hispanic businesspeople are starting companies at four times the rate of all firms? Together, women and minorities comprise nearly 50 percent of all small businesses in the United States. Millions of Americans report for work each day in a company owned by a woman or minority CEO. They pay for their mortgages, children's tuition, and summer vacations with a salary paid by a woman or minority-owned firm.

This book will help you expand your company in size, scope, and influence, whether you are looking for a $1,000 contract or a $100

Breaking Through

million dollar contract. The world of business is changing, and women and minority-owned businesses like yours are on the cutting edge at every level.

As we begin to dig deeper into the supplier diversity landscape, it is important to pause for a moment to define our terms. Thus far I have referred to "women and minority-owned businesses," a somewhat unwieldy phrase that begs the question, what if a business owner is both a woman and a minority? The nation's Latina business owners—a group starting businesses at a whopping six times the rate of all other companies—would certainly question this limiting terminology. Annette Taddeo, a WBENC-certified business owner and the CEO of LanguageSpeak, Inc., resents even the term *minority* and states, "There is nothing minor about me."

Consider this comprehensive list of the current supplier diversity categories. Notice the breadth—and complexity—of the current terminology:

CHEAT SHEET

Supplier Diversity Classifications

- **Minority Business Enterprise (MBE):** A for-profit enterprise currently located in the United States or its trust territories, and is at least 51 percent owned by African Americans, Hispanic Americans, Native Americans, Asian-Indian Americans, and Asian-Pacific Americans. Individual(s) must be involved in the day-to-day management of the business.

- **African Americans** are US citizens whose origins are in any Black racial groups of Africa.

- **Hispanic Americans** are US citizens whose origins are

Introduction

in South America, Central America, Mexico, Cuba, the Dominican Republic, Puerto Rico, or the Iberian Peninsula, including Portugal.

- **Native Americans** are American Indians, Eskimos, Aleuts, and Native Hawaiians.

- **Asian-Indian Americans** are US citizens whose origins are in India, Pakistan, Bangladesh, Sri Lanka, Bhutan, or Nepal.

- **Asian-Pacific Americans** are US citizens whose origins are in Japan, China, the Philippines, Vietnam, Korea, Samoa, Guam, the US Trust Territory of the Pacific Islands (Republic of Palau), the Northern Mariana Islands, Laos, Kampuchea (Cambodia), Taiwan, Burma, Thailand, Malaysia, Indonesia, Singapore, Brunei, Republic of the Marshall Islands, or the Federated States of Micronesia.

- **Woman Business Enterprise (WBE):** A for-profit enterprise currently located in the United States or its trust territories, and is at least 51 percent owned, controlled, and operated by a woman or women of US citizenship. Individual(s) must be involved in the day-to-day management of the business.

- **Disabled Business Enterprise (DBE):** A for-profit enterprise currently located in the United States or its trust territories, and is at least 51 percent owned by an individual(s) of US citizenship with a permanent physical or mental impairment which substantially limits one or more of such persons' major life activities. Individual(s) must be involved in the day-to-day management of the business.

- **Disabled Veteran Business Enterprise (DVE):** A for-profit enterprise currently located in the United States or its trust territories, and is at least 51 percent owned by an individual(s) who have performed active service in one of the United States armed services and is disabled as defined above in DBE. Individual(s) must be involved in the day-to-day management of the business.

- **Veteran Owned Small Business (VOSB):** A small business (as defined pursuant to Section 3 of the Small Business Act) currently located in the United States or its trust territories, and is at least 51 percent owned by an individual(s) who have performed active service in one of the United States armed services.

- **HUBZone (HUB):** A small business located in a HUBZone (Historically Under-utilized Business Zone), owned and controlled by one or more US citizens, with at least 35 percent of its employees residing in a HUBZone. (To learn if you are located in a HUBZone, visit http://map.sba.gov/hubzone/init.asp#address.)

Excerpted from the Citigroup Supplier Diversity website at www.citigroup.com/citigroup/corporate/supplier_diversity/def.htm

Introduction

With WBE (Woman Business Enterprise) certification, you have an extra door open to you in the corporate purchasing process. Of course, this does not guarantee a contract or any special treatment. Your product must be of the highest standards, your price competitive, and your service exemplary. Certification as a WBE is only the beginning.

Breaking Through shares the secrets—the pitches, the proposals, the tips, the marketing plans, the technology platforms—of entrepreneurs who have built successful businesses by including supplier diversity programs in their growth strategy. Their tactics, strategies, successes—and mistakes—will provide you with a blueprint for making supplier diversity work for you. Remember, with over thirteen million women and minority businesses in the United States, there is a lot of competition, so you must differentiate your business, even when you are using the connections and opportunities afforded by supplier diversity contacts.

How do you break through?

Throughout this book, we will ask our panel of expert WBEs whose stories are presented in a case study at the end of each chapter. Let me introduce them:

ABOUT THE CASE STUDY WBEs

Tara Abraham, chairwoman and CEO, Accel inc., is the 2012 chair of WBENC's Women's Enterprise Leadership Forum (The Forum). Accel inc., certified by the Ohio River Valley Women's Business Council (ORVWBC), is the industry leader in hand and automated assembly. The company combines technology and science with creativity to produce the maximum number of products from their production lines flawlessly, on-time, every time. Quality is paramount, inventory control perfect, and innovation unparalleled. Tara says, "If you have a packaging problem, Accel can fix it; we take your headache away." Tara was a Business Star in 2009 and co-chaired the WBENC National Conference and Business Fair in 2009 and 2012 and is WOSB certified.

Rebecca Boenigk is CEO and chairman of the board of Neutral Posture, Inc., and is certified by the Women's Business Enterprise Alliance (WBEA) headquartered in Houston as both a WBE and WOSB. Neutral Posture also holds certifications from DOT, ISO 9001, and WEConnect International. This global company manufactures ergonomic seating and accessories for lab, office, and manufacturing environments. A 2011 Business Star, Rebecca has chaired the Women's Enterprise Leadership Forum (The Forum) and served on the WBENC Board of Directors. Rebecca and her mother, Jaye, began Neutral Posture in 1989 using the pressure-reducing seat design developed by Dr. Jerome Congleton. Neutral Posture is now a top diversity supplier for the US government and Fortune 500 companies worldwide.

Cathi Coan is the mother of four and owner of Techway Services, Inc. Techway has provided end-of-life (EOL) IT services for corporations, government entities, universities, and channel partners. A Business Star in 2012 and member of The Forum, Cathi is certified by the Women's Business Council Southwest (WBCS) and will be adding WEConnect certification for her new Canadian division in the near future. Cathi is committed to the highest standards both as a mother and as a business owner. Growing up in a small Texas town, Cathi learned the value of integrity and building a good reputation early. Those same values are evident in her commitment to her clients, to her company's business standards, and to the planet. Cathi is currently treasurer for the Electronic Resource Recovery Council of the Recycling Alliance of Texas, and is on the board of the Greater Dallas Fort Worth Recycling Alliance.

Patty Klein is president and CEO of A-Plus Meetings & Incentives, the thirtieth-largest event management firm in the country, with $14 million in tier-1 spend. Certified by the Women's

Introduction

Business Development Council of Florida (WBDC-Florida), A-Plus Meetings & Incentives also holds WOSB certification. Patty was a Business Star in 2011 and has managed the WBENC Salute and Summit since 2010. She was also selected as an Ernst & Young's "Entrepreneurial Winning Women" in 2011. A-Plus provides full-service meeting planning and incentive travel services for Fortune 500 companies, such as Staples, DHL, and Ryder. The firm has an exceptional track record of high service and repeat customers and provides unique value-add on both content and negotiations. Their successful methodology is driven by the management team, who hold MBAs from Harvard and Wharton Business schools and who previously were consultants with McKinsey and Bain prior to creating A-Plus.

Ranjini Poddar is president of Artech Information Systems, LLC, certified by the Women Presidents' Education Organization New York (WPEO-NY). Artech also holds ISO 27000, ISO 9001, LEED, and NMSDC certifications. The recipient of numerous awards and recognition, Ranjini is a member of the WBENC Board of Directors and the co-chair of both the 2009 and 2013 National Conference and Business Fair. Artech is a global enterprise that provides workforce solutions to over sixty Fortune and Global 500 companies.

Janet Crenshaw Smith is president of Ivy Planning Group, LLC, a full-service management consulting firm. Certified by the Women Presidents' Educational Organization DC, Ivy Planning Group (IVY) specializes in diversity and inclusion training. It also provides strategy, change management, and leadership development. Founded in 1990, IVY has received numerous awards and developed a distinguished reputation with Fortune 1000 companies, large nonprofits, and government agencies. Janet says, "Our passion is balancing strategy, diversity, and the bottom line by leveraging differences in the workforce, workplace, and marketplace opportunity. Everything we do is designed to enhance our clients' ability to implement diversity."

Camilla Sullivan is principal of Visionista, a content management and production company that truly understands brand strategy, design, web best practices, complex value propositions, and industrial strength messaging. Camilla infuses this creative agency with more than fifteen years of global marketing, communications, and analyst experience from working with Fortune 500 companies on brand strategies, product launches, new market development, and marketing strategy. Of their several divisions and many capabilities, Camilla says, "Visionista Productions is a video and original content production agency built on proven storytelling techniques fused with cutting-edge marketing and communications expertise. We deliver complete and effective campaigns—from integrated online campaigns to full television production." The company, certified by the Women Presidents Educational Organization-DC (WPEO-DC), has received many prestigious industry awards, including Stevie 2012 Silver and Gold recognition.

Cindy Funaro Towers is president and CEO of JuriSolutions, the parent company of CYLA, JuriStaff, and JXP Search, certified by the Women's Business Development Center PA-DE-sNJ (WBDC PA-DE-sNJ). Together these divisions specialize in the innovative and cost-efficient delivery of high-quality legal services and the building of successful legal teams. JXP performs executive searches for legal and managerial positions; JuriStaff provides interim legal and government staffing; and CYLA provides legal services from more than 150 specialized attorneys across the country. In addition to WOSB certification, Cindy holds certifications from the City of Philadelphia, the States of Pennsylvania, Delaware, and New Jersey, and the California Public Utility Commission. She is a 2013 Business Star.

Nancy Williams and her partner, Roz Alford, are principals of ASAP Solutions Group, LLC, certified by the Greater Women's Business Council (GWBC). A past chair of The Forum, Nancy was a Business Star in 2008. ASAP is a privately held, women-owned corporation that has enjoyed strong, steady growth since 1989. It

Introduction

is among the largest women-owned firms in the state of Georgia and were ranked number eight on *Atlanta Business Chronicle*'s Top 25 Women-Owned Businesses in 2011. The company's competencies are IT consulting and solutions, managed services, IT staff augmentation, and work compliance. ASAP has over eight hundred consultants on staff with an average of eight years of professional experience. Nancy says, "The key to our success has been to establish strong partnerships with our clients, including many Fortune 100 firms as well as the federal, state, and local governments." In addition to offices in Atlanta, Chicago, Dallas, and New Jersey, ASAP has an offshore facility in Hyderabad, India.

WHAT WE WILL COVER

In chapter one, you will learn everything there is to know about supplier diversity programs: what they are, who runs them, how long they have been around, and how you, the entrepreneur, can find them in your industry. The best supplier diversity programs include outreach to MWBEs, information on how to do business with a corporation, assistance in identifying the correct departmental buyer and the appropriate timing for a marketing call. But every program is different. Interviews with representatives from some of America's leading companies will provide you with an insider's view of how these departments really work across a broad array of industries and how they want to work with you.

Next, in chapter two, you will learn the essential first building block to supplying corporate America: certification. Supplier diversity programs usually require that you be certified as a women or as a minority business enterprise, validating that your company is 51 percent owned, operated, and controlled by a woman or minority. They rely on independent, third-party organizations such as the Women's Business Enterprise National Council (WBENC) to conduct the certification process. This chapter provides a concise and easy-to-understand explanation of how you can obtain and maintain your certification as a WBE and a WOSB. The process will be reviewed and a checklist provided for the documents you should organize before starting the certification process.

Chapter three provides information on targeting your marketing strategy to take full advantage of your WBE status. This chapter will share the marketing plans and outreach strategies of successful certified businesses.

In real estate, they say, "Location, location, location." For business owners, the chant is "Network, network, network." Chapter four of *Breaking Through* shows you how and tells you where. Attendance at business fairs and buyers' marts (sponsored by women's or minority business organizations and corporations) provide access to purchasing professionals who want to buy from you—not sell to you, as is true at many other trade fairs and conferences. Relationships are crucial to M/WBE success, and networking is the way to build strong contacts.

Chapter five offers advanced strategies for certified businesses, such as strategic alliances and second-tier supplying. This chapter explains the many doors available for suppliers wanting to do business with corporate America so readers can explore every possible opportunity.

Chapters six, seven, and eight explore the three Ps of supplier diversity: preparation, pitching, and perseverance. In chapter 6, interviews with representatives from some of America's leading companies will provide you with an insider's view of how these departments really work across a broad array of industries and how they want to work with you. Advice from corporate supplier diversity professionals, leaders of our RPOs and WBEs, will help you prepare to ask and answer the right questions to win business from a large corporation. This includes establishing your pricing and knowing your technological capabilities.

Chapter seven discusses the second P, pitching. This chapter outlines the importance of developing and practicing key messages to seal the deal. Remember, you may have only a few minutes to explain what your business does and why the person you are speaking with should be interested. Experts provide tips on how to create presentations that distinguish your product or service from the competition and comfortably incorporate your MWBE status into your sales pitch.

Chapter eight shares several stories of the perseverance and patience required to do business with corporate America. For go-go entrepreneurs, this can be the most challenging aspect of the process.

Finally, chapter nine of *Breaking Through* will help you keep the contracts you secure. Making the client's goals your goals is key to building long-term relationships and long-term success.

Breaking Through: Creating Opportunities for America's Women and Minority-Owned Businesses is your partner in business growth. It can be read and reread at every stage of your company's development, from start-up to becoming a Fortune 1000 business. Refer to the stories, tips, and checklists on the following pages whenever you find yourself at a crossroads or in need of support and inspiration.

The goal of this book is to help businesses like yours achieve the amazing expansion of which you are capable. *Breaking Through* will help make you and your company the big business success story of the next decade.

Chapter One
Big Bucks from Big Business

If you are a woman or minority business owner, there is no greater opportunity to grow your business than to access the corporate market. This holds true no matter what product or service you offer and no matter how big or small your company. The best news of all is that if you take advantage of the recommendations in this book and become involved in corporate supplier diversity programs and certification organizations, you will find enormous support along the way.

Whether you are entirely new to supplier diversity or you are a certified pro, this chapter provides an essential overview of the ever-growing supplier diversity industry. I will share an insider's guide to the "who, what, when, where, why and how" of corporate supplier diversity programs. You should master the information in this chapter before you approach any company as a potential vendor.

FAQ: Could my company really win a contract with a large corporation?

Women and minority business owners new to the world of supplier diversity are often surprised at the range of businesses—from sole proprietorships to multimillion-dollar companies—supplying to large corporations through this exciting door to opportunity. Through our case studies and success stories, you will meet women who run companies that provide products and services as diverse as promotional items, high-tech business solutions, packaging, meeting management, legal services, staffing, diversity consulting, and more.

Why is There a Need for Supplier diversity Programs?

One of our founding corporate board members, Jerry Martin, who was at the time senior vice president of Global Purchasing for Frito-Lay, said it best: "As large company buyers, we set up barriers that we do not even know we are raising. We have to make a special effort to go beyond doing business as usual. Supplier diversity programs are the way we make certain the barriers come down."

As defined in the introduction, supplier diversity programs are corporate initiatives to create mutually beneficial business relationships between previously disadvantaged businesses (those of women, ethnic minority, and disabled business owners) and large corporations that can purchase their products and services. While many companies have a lot of catching up to do, at least 350 of the Fortune 500 are eager to do business with diverse suppliers like you and support WBENC initiatives on the national and regional levels.

Long-time corporate leader Cheryl Stevens, vice president of supplier diversity for Energy Future Holdings Corporation and past chair of the board of WBENC, sees an uptick in support from corporate America based on a refined understanding of the business case. "Companies have realized the value of certification and of the WBEs," she says. "They understand the business reason. Corporate America has realized that in no way has the commitment to diversity ever been driven by quotas or set-asides or handouts. It has been about the recognition that corporations have the opportunity to be more successful in reaching their goals because they have significant stakeholders out there that help them to reach those goals."

Supplier diversity departments exist because smart corporations know that the demographics of the American economic landscape have changed dramatically; they must do business with the diverse groups that represent their supplier and customer base today and into the future. Besides the fact that women and minorities are starting businesses at a rapid pace, we are also growing by leaps and bounds in number and in consumer power. Corporate America cannot afford to lose our business.

At the 2013 Top Corporation panel at the WBENC Summit and Salute, William Hawthorne, Macy's vice president of diversity strategies and legal, told the audience, "It is a no-brainer when you think about our customer, which is 70 percent female. We need to connect and engage, and develop customer loyalty. Our workforce is almost 70 percent female as well."

Consider these numbers: American women overall spend more than $3.7 trillion a year, making them the largest consumer nation in the world.

Why am I so passionate about the opportunity for MWBEs to do business with corporate America? Because we can! The numbers prove that we are only at the tip of the iceberg. For example, American Express OPEN's third *State of Women-Owned Businesses Report in 2013* included detailed analysis of data from the US Census Bureau, offering updated estimates of the number of women-owned firms nationally and in all fifty states plus the District of Columbia. It compares the growth rates of women-owned businesses from 1997 through 2013. New to the 2013 report was a look at the remarkable growth in the number and economic clout of firms owned by women of color. Here are some of the most important findings in this report:

> • The number and economic contributions of women-owned firms continue to grow. The rate of growth in the number of women-owned enterprises over the past sixteen years remains higher than the national average. Between 1997 and 2013, the number of women-owned firms is growing at one and a half times the national average.

• Over the past six years, since the depth of the US recession, the only businesses that have provided a net increase in employment are large, publicly traded corporations ... and privately held majority women-owned firms. In all other privately held firms, employment has declined over the 2007–2013 period.

• Since 1997, the growth in the number and economic contributions of firms owned by women of color is nothing short of remarkable. Comprising just 17 percent of women-owned firms sixteen years ago, firms owned by women of color now account for one in three women-owned firms in the United States.

• Comparing trends in the number and revenue accomplishments of women-owned and all firms by industries finds that women-owned firms are exceeding overall sector growth in eight of the thirteen most populous industries. In two of those industries (construction and transportation) women business owners are standing toe to toe with their competitors in terms of revenue accomplishments.

• The states with the fastest growth in the number, employment, and revenues of women-owned firms are the District of Columbia, North Dakota, Nevada, Wyoming, and Georgia. The fastest growing metropolitan areas for women-owned firms are San Antonio TX, Portland OR, Houston TX, Riverside CA, and Washington DC/MD/VA.

THE RIGHT STUFF

Some companies are getting it right when it comes to supplier diversity. More and more companies improve their standards for supplier diversity every day, and it is worth noting which companies are making an effort to create a strong supplier diversity program when you are deciding which corporations to target as prospects. Look to the WBENC website for news on corporations implementing new programs and companies excelling with existing programs. WBENC presents America's Top Corporations for America's Women's Business Enterprises annually (Top Corps). Affiliates of WBENC honor companies on a regional level as well. Cheryl Stevens advises to "look around at the tables [at a WBENC event] and see the names of the sponsors and see the banners on the walls. While there is a spectrum of performance, they have said 'we believe in that concept enough to put some bucks on the table.' We don't have to say who is doing a bad job, because we say who is doing a good job."

In one of those Top Corporations, United Airlines' Katrina Manning, vice president of technical procurement, says, "It is easy for programs to get lost. This is not a program for us—it is part of our business plan. Director of Supplier Diversity Ruby McCleary did a deep dive with our board. We placed supplier diversity in procurement where buying decisions are made. What gets measured gets managed. We review our results monthly. Supplier diversity requires not a department but a passion."

WHAT DEFINES A CORPORATE SUPPLIER DIVERSITY PROGRAM?

Corporate supplier diversity programs, departments, and initiatives vary from company to company, but their function is to serve as internal advocates for women and minority suppliers. Consider the mission statement of the UPS Supplier diversity Program:

> We provide access and equal opportunity to diverse suppliers and promote and develop these suppliers within and outside our organization. We are committed to ensuring that our Supplier diversity Process strengthens the small, minority and woman owned businesses that drive economic development in the communities we serve.

Big Bucks from Big Business

As you can see, the goal of UPS and other corporate supplier diversity programs is to *help you succeed.* Specifically, supplier diversity programs incorporate a combination of the following elements:

Outreach—Corporate supplier diversity professionals actively seek relationships with diverse suppliers like you. They find WBEs through involvement with business development organizations (see chapter four for more details on various associations and networking groups), participation in various business fair activities and creation and maintenance of informational websites that solicit diverse suppliers. Often they identify appropriate MWBEs as soon as they hear of a Request for Proposal (RFP) somewhere in their organization.

Certification—Corporations verify that businesses seeking to participate in their supplier diversity programs meet the criteria of ownership, management, and control to qualify for their initiatives. Many companies offer certification workshops and training or partner with recognized certifying organizations like WBENC to help facilitate the certification process. (The next chapter will walk you through the certification process in detail.) Ernst & Young has taken it a step further. Susan O'Rourke, director of America's Procurement, says,

> Women entrepreneurs are a vital source in this economy. They own 46 percent of all businesses and provide sixteen million jobs. Yet the 54 percent of male-owned companies are far more likely to reach a million in revenue. We created the *Entrepreneurial Winning Women* program to address this problem. We make our firm's resources available and provide mentors and education while creating networks into which they can tap in and grow. We have five key themes:
>
> - Think big and be bold.
> - Take advantage of media—create your public image.
> - Work on your business not just in your business.

- Create networks—in and out of your industry,
- Evaluate financial opportunities to scale to the next level.

Qualification—Supplier diversity staff review the capabilities of MWBE businesses and refer them to appropriate purchasers for consideration as suppliers.

Development—They also review additional needs of MWBE suppliers and explore ways to provide assistance to them through training, education, and sometimes formal mentoring. Supplier diversity professionals help MWBEs define their value propositions, often advising them on how to better manage cost, margin, and price variables.

Utilization—Supplier diversity staff participate in the purchasing process, partnering with purchasing managers in the department needing your product or service. For example, if you are a temporary staffing company, your supplier diversity contact would facilitate your relationship with the company's human resources department and other specific areas that need temporary workers. IT staffing in particular has become a major area of opportunity for MWBEs.

Tracking—Supplier diversity departments monitor and report on supplier diversity practices to achieve the company's targets and continually improve results. Companies with "the right stuff" set goals for their diversity initiatives that must be met on annually. Typically, today's corporations utilize sophisticated databases that "scrub" procurement lists to identify which of their current and prospective suppliers are women or minority owned and what certifications those companies hold.

Progressive companies monitor their success in supplier diversity through various benchmarking procedures. Through its annual Top Corporations awards program, WBENC actively supports tracking so we can guide certified WBEs to committed companies, and encourage other companies to improve their practices.

How Do I Decide Which Corporations to Target?

Tip #1: Look for customers committed to supplier diversity.

As you are beginning to see, some corporations are more committed to supplier diversity than others. I highly recommend that you begin your process of targeting potential corporate customers by researching which companies foster strong supplier diversity programs. These are the companies that will be most receptive to the strategies outlined in this book.

How do you begin to research corporations that might be customers for your products or services? The first point of entry I always recommend is the Internet. Virtually every corporate supplier diversity department in the country offers an informative website that tells you most of what you need to know to make your initial approach. It is a good idea to visit as many supplier diversity websites as possible to review various program structures. The more information you can gather, the better.

Marianne Strobel of AT&T says,

> I encourage WBEs to register in our Prospective Supplier Database, but only after they review the Opportunity Areas section of our website. If WBEs do not see their product or service listed, then they may not be pursuing the right market for their company. I can appreciate the time it takes for WBEs to develop new business, so we do everything we can to be clear where our opportunities are and are not. Supplier profiles from our database are used frequently by our team, so it is important to be 'on our radar' if a WBE offers what we list as a need area.

I also recommend using search engines such as Google, entering keywords from your business (for example, software, marketing, electrical components, administrative services, and so on) and the term "supplier diversity."

As we will explore in chapter three, corporate supplier diversity websites feature lists of what, when, and how they buy from MWBEs. I recommend compiling a notebook or individual files containing information and notes about each company's supplier diversity program so you can keep track of your prospects. Some websites offer downloadable reports and information that may be easier to digest offline. It is also smart to keep a list of MWBE suppliers featured as "success stories" (a popular feature of many supplier diversity websites), as you may want to contact some of the owners of those businesses as you progress through the process of becoming a supplier.

This does not work for every company. Cyndi Hopkins, director of Global Supplier Diversity at Dell advises, "Typically, we do not list procurement opportunities on the website. We encourage suppliers to contact our supplier diversity team to learn about upcoming opportunities. We tell suppliers interested in doing business with Dell to be pleasantly persistent and to understand where they fit in the supply chain and the importance of timing. We want to ensure our WBE suppliers are identified for the right opportunity."

Tip #2: Get involved early and often.

The Internet is a necessary and helpful first step in your research, but you must accompany your online efforts with offline ones. While much of the supplier diversity process now takes place online (see later chapters on certification and technology), face-to-face interaction is still a significant component of the purchasing process. Cindy Tower, president and CEO of JuriSolutions says, "My first WBENC conference was in San Francisco. With the help of my regional partner organization president, Geri Swift, I was able to accomplish more in terms of marketing my company than I had done in the past ten years. Geri asked who I wanted to meet and proceeded to make the introductions."

WBENC events also proved to be a good opportunity for Cathi Coan of Techway Services. "I saw Howard Thompson from Macy's at the Summit and Salute in 2012, and he put me in contact with the right purchasing manager. We have worked with them at six different Macy's locations since our last conversation."

The best way to research supplier diversity opportunities offline is to become involved with one of the many organizations that provide educational and networking opportunities for MWBEs.

According to Kim Brown of Dell,

> It is imperative for any potential supplier pursuing business with Dell to have an understanding of Dell's business strategy and how their company supports that strategy. Leverage social media, Twitter, Facebook, and LinkedIn to follow discussions on Dell, as well as the vast amount of information published to ensure that you are relevant when demonstrating your company's value proposition. Take advantage of the opportunities to build relationships with our supplier diversity team, our primes, and the minority/women/small businesses already doing business with Dell at national and regional partner events. Our strategy begins with serving our customers' evolving needs. We are looking for suppliers that will help us to deliver the technology solutions that enable people everywhere to grow and thrive, simplify our portfolio, and actively listen to our customers.

Chapter four will recommend many strategies for networking in the supplier diversity community, but your first stop should be your regional partner organization affiliate of WBENC. While you may already be a member of your industry association, many MWBEs have never connected with the supplier diversity factions of their membership organizations. Ask your association contacts to introduce you to any supplier diversity or procurement professionals in the organization as you begin to explore this new business opportunity.

To find even more face-to-face opportunities, pay close attention to calendar listings on the corporate websites you are researching. As mentioned above, many companies' missions include extensive outreach to potential suppliers, so they regularly sponsor information sessions and business fairs to provide opportunities for you to meet their staff, purchasing executives, successful MWBE suppliers, nonprofit partners, and other experienced professionals who can help you through the process. It is true: companies offer events to educate you on how to sell to them. If you are certified by WBENC and keep your online profile up-to-date, you will receive this information as a matter of course. Other associations provide similar informational services as well.

Do not forget to log the information you gather at live events in your trusty notebook or digital folder containing your Internet research. Be sure to take copious notes; all of this information will be useful as you navigate the supplier diversity process.

Who Works in the Supplier diversity Field?

The supplier diversity field is a professional industry like any other, with experienced practitioners doing their jobs day in and day out. I have talked to some of the top men and women in the field in order to understand the supplier diversity process from their point of view: what their workday looks like; what they look for in a supplier; what impresses them; what annoys them; and what you can do to build a strong relationship with them. Their advice and success secrets appear throughout this book.

To succeed as a supplier, you will need to develop close, trusting relationships with the supplier diversity staff at the companies you target. Purchasing professionals regularly cite "strong relationships" as one of the leading success factors for MWBE suppliers. Supplier diversity managers truly are your allies in the corporate purchasing process. With all that is said about high tech these days, "high touch" is still important in building business relationships, and supplier diversity is no exception.

In fact, I truly believe that the single most important success factor for MWBEs is the building and maintaining of relationships with supplier diversity professionals. Supplier diversity executives' jobs are to find qualified diverse suppliers for their companies needs and advocate on behalf of *you* in the corporate purchasing process. The better your relationship with these advocates, the better your chance of being in the front of their mind when new contracts arise. Do not just take my word for it. WBENC's surveys have found that 97 percent of women entrepreneur respondents rated relationships with decision makers as a key success factor in doing business with large corporations.

Sandra Eberhard, executive director of WPEO-DC agrees. "We hold a panel discussion each year that used to be called 'I am Certified Now What?' that was targeted to newly certified companies. Its success, and the knowledge imparted to participants, has led us to the conclusion that it benefits all certified WBEs." A panel includes at least four supplier diversity professionals.

Sandra also says, "I want the business owners to understand the value of the professional and what they can do for them in the company. It is not just getting the contract, although a good relationship is tantamount to getting the contract. The supplier diversity professional can help the WBE understand the corporate culture, and if they get the contract, can help them to build long-term relationships within the company."

Many corporations also have purchasing councils and supplier diversity advocates throughout the supply chain to further advocate on your behalf. The supplier diversity executive is in regular contact with these additional individuals, knows what they are looking for and can provide you with fast-lane access to the appropriate buyer. Sandra adds, "Supplier diversity executives network across companies and share information about their most successful MWBE suppliers."

A Day in the Life

It is important to understand the roles and responsibilities of supplier diversity executives so you can help them achieve their goals. While responsibilities vary depending on the level and experience of the executive, consider these elements that might be found in the position description of a supplier diversity executive:

- Identify and build relationships with qualified, diverse suppliers to recommend them to purchasers across the corporation. (Many supplier diversity professionals travel extensively to conferences, trade shows, seminars, award banquets, association meetings and activities, presentations, and face-to-face meetings with WBE suppliers.)
- Sit on the boards or committees of various local, national, and regional certification organizations as well as associations, councils, and WBE businesses.
- Respond to MWBE inquiries, and work with them to provide education on the needs of the corporation and the requirements for becoming a supplier, including the importance of certification (see chapter two). Provide mentoring and advice as appropriate.
- Train corporate purchasing personnel across the corporation in the need to include MWBEs as suppliers.
- Obtain requirements from prime (first-tier) contractors to facilitate second-tier opportunities for MWBEs (see chapter five for more information about second-tier supplying).
- Manage the supplier diversity website and other program-marketing collateral.

- Track the results of your supplier diversity program to meet the company's goals, as set by your company's CEO and senior management.

CHEAT SHEET

GETTING TO KNOW YOUR SUPPLIER DIVERSITY CONTACTS

Be sure to find out the following information about any supplier diversity professional at the companies you target, and keep this information updated as you move through the process:

- Name: (Never misspell the name of someone you are trying to impress.)

- Title: (Be sure to get this right as well. Titles vary from company to company and change frequently.)

- Company:

- Contact information:

- Preferred method of communication: (E-mail, phone, cell phone?)

- Assistant's name:

- Areas of responsibility: (What internal departments, geographic regions, and/or ethnic markets does this person oversee? Again, responsibilities vary by company.)

- Name of regional or local contact person (if different from above):

Center for Women and Enterprise President and CEO Susan Rittscher offers the following list of don'ts when dealing with supplier diversity contacts in the companies you have targeted:

DON'TS FOR WBES

What *not* to do:

- *Don't* start a conversation before doing your homework; understand requirements, what they sell, their operations, their locations.
- *Don't* e-mail around the whole corporation after the supplier diversity manager has already provided guidance.
- *Don't* send mass distribution e-mails instead of personalized e-mails.
- *Don't* talk negatively about your competition rather than talking positively about your company.
- *Don't* tell a company you can save 20 percent versus what they're paying with vendor X, when you have no idea what their cost structure is.
- *Don't* submit incomplete or sloppy RFPs or packets; understand the required documents for your industry.
- *Don't* assign an inexperienced sales rep.
- *Don't* have unrealistic expectations; relationship building takes time.
- *Don't* lose patience.

But at the same time ...

Don't push when you've already been told no. Also, don't burn bridges if the ultimate result ends up in rejection or lack of response.

When Do Companies Make Their Purchases from Diverse Suppliers?

Purchasing schedules vary from company to company and product to product, so you will need to research timing with each company you choose to target. I will say, however, that selling to corporate America can be a very long process—lasting from several months to several years—but, as the following chapters will demonstrate, the rewards are well worth the wait.

Nancy Williams, co-president of ASAP Solutions Group, says, "My partner, Roz, and I go to every event both regionally and nationally. You never know who you are going to meet, but you won't meet anyone if you don't show up. The relationships may take five years or more; people do business with people they trust. Products are products are products. Building relationships is a long-term strategy. They want to make certain you have their back." (See the full case study on Nancy and her company at the end of chapter nine.)

I encourage you to be aggressive, but also to be patient.

Where Do I Get Started?

The best way to launch your company into the world of supplier diversity is to become certified. The next chapter will show you how. According to WBE Lois Gamerman,

> I found that being WBENC certified was a great asset, because it proved that my company, Soft Stuff Distributors, was truly a woman-owned business. This assisted me greatly is getting the "ear" of the diversity supply manager, but it was not enough. Through my networking with other WBENC members, I learned how important it was to register on the websites of every company that I was interested in doing business with. I immediately registered with Sodexo, Inc., and the net result of this was being immediately contacted by the National Zoo and

Breaking Through

given the opportunity to provide them with a customized fresh baked cookie program. This then led to expanded business with them and referrals to other Sodexo-managed foodservice facilities.

Barbara Bosha of Bosha Design + Communications offers another testament to the payoff of registering on corporate sites: "Because of WBENC, I was encouraged to register on corporate website diversity portals. I did, and a person from Supply Chain, Johnson & Johnson found me there. I had never met the person, but because of the portal, the buyers knew where to look. That happened in November 2007, and I have been doing work for them ever since."

CASE STUDY

CINDY FUNARO TOWERS, ESQ., JURISOLUTIONS

The daughter of entrepreneurs that experienced the trials of the Depression, Cindy had a strong work ethic. Cindy worked first as a nurse and then s an attorney, but her focus changed to business ownership when she had to cancel her honeymoon because the judge for the case on which she was working would not change the date of the trial. "I was not lead counsel but had done most of the work on the case," Cindy said. "Sacrifice is worthwhile, but on this trial I was not saving lives—just saving a lot of money for the insurance company we were representing."

Legal staffing was not her first idea. "It was the time when theme restaurants were popular—Hard Rock Cafe and others. I had a business plan all written for my restaurant 'Barrestaurers' when my brother convinced me that it was not the best idea. I had used temporary legal help for some of my trials, and my business partner and I were both lawyers, so it made sense that in 1997 we started a legal staffing company."

Cindy and her cofounder sold a part of the company in 2000 to a part to woman attorney and part to her mother and became women-owned. What started as a traditional staffing company now has three divisions that provide temporary legal staffing, executive search, and specialized legal services.

They were aware of WBENC and had actually looked at the application but had not yet applied for certification when they had the opportunity to get an appointment with a purchasing official from WBENC corporate member GlaxoSmithKline. Marty Harlow in legal procurement suggested it would help in the RFP process if they were certified, as there were many suppliers applying for the company's temporary lawyers to be assigned to a specific litigation. GlaxoSmithKline had decided to approach suppliers directly instead of going through their outside legal counsel, as they had done in the past.

"We explained that we were women-owned but did not have certification. We thought it would be a daunting process," Cindy said. "We did it for them."

And it worked. Two firms split the award, including JuriSolutions, which was at that time a $7-million business and a mega player in the space, with revenues upward of $1 billion. Cindy and her team knew that getting certified and getting the contract were only first steps in developing a long-term client.

Cindy continues the story: "Two years into the contract, the continuation was rebid. We had outperformed this behemoth company at every turn. When the contract was up for renewal, we alone were selected. This proves the WBENC story: as a WBE, you can get the opportunity at bat, but to succeed you need to knock it out of the park."

Chapter Two

Becoming Certified

The History of Certification

Supplier diversity officially entered the American business landscape in 1968, when the US Small Business Administration (SBA) established a program to channel some government purchases to "disadvantaged" owners of small businesses. The following year, a presidential order established the Office of Minority Business Enterprise within the Commerce Department to oversee this initiative. In 1972, the National Minority Supplier Development Council (NMSDC) was founded to certify businesses as minority-owned.

Many private-sector supplier diversity programs were, in fact, originally created to identify minority-owned businesses and only later added women to the list of eligible companies. Part of the problem was the lack of a nationally recognized certification for women business enterprises, a void that WBENC filled with our creation of WBE certification in 1997.

When WBENC was putting together its first group of stakeholders to launch the first nationally accepted certification program for women business enterprises, Carol Dougal was an important expert at the table. The Women's Business Development Center, based in Chicago and led by Carol and her co-president Hedy Ratner, had been certifying for a few years in the Chicagoland area. Formed to provide education and support for women entrepreneurs, WBDC was encouraged to add certification to their offerings by the local minority council, led by May Foster Thompson. The council, while recognizing the importance of certification for women and for

Becoming Certified

the corporations served by the council, did not want to do it themselves. Carol reports,

> A representative from Allstate became chair of our certification group, and we modeled our process on that of the NMSDC and its chapters. Once we became part of WBENC, our process and implementation became more stringent. The rules were similar—almost identical—but the application was more stringent.
>
> We have seen positive change over the years. In the beginning we worried about getting the big women-owned businesses to get certified. Now they are clamoring to get certified. At first we were twisting their arms, and now it is like a club they want to be in.

Today WBENC certification is widely accepted and just as widely respected for its rigorous standards and consistent procedures.

Certification organizations such as WBENC provide corporations with a way to verify that companies qualify for their supplier diversity programs as 51 percent owned, operated, and controlled by a woman. Hundreds of local, regional, and national government agencies also provide certification. As mentioned earlier, certification is by no means a guarantee of a corporate contract, but it is a necessary first step toward supplier diversity opportunities.

Can certification be a complicated and time-consuming process? Yes, sometimes. Even attorney Cindy Tower at first thought it would be a daunting process. Becoming certified is by no means easy, but this is one of the reasons corporations respect the qualification so deeply and why supplier diversity professionals are so committed to helping certified businesses succeed. They know that a business owner who has successfully completed the demanding certification process is motivated, organized, and ambitious.

Additionally, many certified businesses report that they learned invaluable information about themselves, their businesses, and the supplier diversity marketplace while navigating the certification process. *Now it is your turn to get started.*

WANT TO BE A MILLION-DOLLAR BUSINESS? GET CERTIFIED!

According to a study conducted on behalf of WBENC by the Center for Women's Business Research, women-owned $1-million firms are nearly two and a half times as likely as other women-owned businesses to be certified as a WBE.

THE STEPS TO CERTIFICATION

Step One: Learn the requirements for various certifications and decide which one is right for you.

Approximate time: one to two weeks.

There are four major criteria for certification by WBENC as a WBE. Review this list and be sure you are a qualified applicant before you begin the process:

- At least 51 percent ownership by a woman or women
- Proof of effective management of the business (operating position, bylaws, hire-fire, and other decision-making roles)
- Control of the business as evidenced by signature authority on loans, leases, and contracts
- US citizenship (WBENC, but not all certifying agencies, also provides certification to those able to verify US resident alien status)

Federal government certifications also include requirements that your business meet certain size standards and that you fall under certain ceilings of personal net worth. Some government certifications still require proof that you are "disadvantaged." To meet this particular criterion, you must establish that you have been discriminated against economically and socially. If you are a member of certain ethnic minorities detailed in chapter one, you are considered to be included in a "presumed class" and automatically meet those criteria. Nonminority women must make an individual case of societal discrimination by putting forward documentation on such experiences as the denial of credit, exclusion from educational opportunities, or discriminatory hiring practices.

WOSB CERTIFICATION

The US Small Business Administration (SBA) has approved WBENC as a third-party certifier for Women-Owned Small Business (WOSB) certification as part of the SBA's WOSB Federal Contracting Program.

President and CEO of WBENC Pamela Prince-Eason says, "This is a historical moment as WBENC advances its mission of leveling the playing field for women business enterprises not only in the private sector, but now in the public sector. We are pleased that the US SBA, like our current corporate partners, recognizes the value and credibility of third-party certification. Through the approval of third-party certification, the SBA has taken an important step in enabling women's businesses to compete effectively and win contracts with the government. We believe that this will lead to women's business growth and a positive impact on our economy."

Application for WOSB certification can be submitted with a new application, recertification application and any time prior to recertification. To move forward, please ensure you meet the criteria then follow the steps below that apply to your particular circumstance.

CRITERIA FOR CERTIFICATION AS A WOSB

- The applicant company must be "small" in its primary industry in accordance with SBA's size standards for that industry. Please view the listing of NAICS and their size standards for verification, available at www.wbenc.org.
- The applicant company must be at least 51 percent unconditionally and directly owned and controlled by one or more women who are US citizens.
- Management and daily operation must be controlled by one or more of the women owners.
- The women owners must make long-term decisions for the business.
- One of the criteria below must also be true for *corporations only*:
    - Women must make up a majority of the board of directors *or* have a majority of the board votes through weighted voting.
    - Women must make up 51 percent of the voting power, sit on the board, *and* have enough voting power to overcome any supermajority requirement.

WBENC uses a two-part process to ensure that the applicant company meets the WBENC WOSB standards. This will include a thorough review of the documentation presented and a site visit interview with the female owner(s).

Additional requirements:

- Applicant must possess a DUNS number.
- Applicant must be registered in SAM (System for Award Management).

Documentation required:

- Copy of WOSB application.
- Proof of registration in www.sam.gov.

- One of the following documents must be submitted:
    - Printout of first page of IRS Form 941 (for previous four quarters)
    - W-3 from previous year
    - Current list of employees (*only* if the previous two items do not apply to our company)
    - If you are a sole owner of the applicant company, provide a statement listing yourself as the only employee

Michelle Richards, president of the Women's Business Enterprise Council–Great Lakes, advises that obtaining WOSB certification pays off. "Local business owner Mary Marble of Marble Mechanical Services attended the WBEC-Great Lakes 2012 Leadership Institute for Women. The one-day training focused on improving your bid package. With staff assistance, Mary then registered for the EDWOSB certification. In November 2012, she received a multimillion-dollar federal contract for her HVAC company."

Step 1: Should I apply for more than one certification?

By all means! While it takes time and effort to apply for multiple certifications, you will increase your exposure to corporate and government contracts by applying for all the certifications for which you are eligible. Some customers will even insist that you have a specific certification for their industry or region. As you have learned already, the most common national certifications include WBENC (for women business enterprises), NMSDC (for minority business enterprises), and various government certifications for all of the categories listed in chapter one. Note the information provided in the introduction on our case study WBEs to see the certifications they each hold.

If you have questions, the answer may be as close as your RPO. Susan Rittscher, president of the Center for Women & Enterprise, says, "In 2013, CWE will provide three sessions (in different regional areas) in conjunction with the SBA and New England states in order to provide information on the different certification options and benefits."

Leslie Saunders, WBENC-certified CEO of Leslie Saunders Insurance and Marketing, and Simplify Benefits, currently holds over fifty certifications, most of them as a DBE—disadvantaged business enterprise. One of Leslie's early customers was Budget Rent-A-Car, which requested that she acquire local certification to fulfill the requirements of their local-government airport contracts. Budget began to send her applications from airport cities across the country, each of which required its own certification.

Leslie hired a college intern whose entire job consisted of sorting through the certification process and assembling each application. The intern organized it all, and Leslie's business started getting certified—and getting business—all over the country. Maintaining those certifications and keeping abreast of changing requirements on the federal and state levels are an important concern for her business.

When I first met Leslie, the number of her certifications was over one hundred; fortunately, changes in policy from the Federal Aviation Administration and Department of Transportation have helped to consolidate many of these individual certifications into regional and state certifications. Leslie still maintains her dozens and dozens of certifications in addition to her WBENC certification. "I hope I live to see the day when I will need only one national certification—WBENC—that is accepted everywhere," she says. We agree.

Becoming Certified

Step 2: Visit the website of the organization(s) providing the certification(s) for which you plan to apply.

WBENC certification begins online at www.wbenc.org/certification. I will use it as a model for navigating the online application process.

Step one on the web is to set yourself up with a user account. This is quite similar to many other popular Internet sites, such as eBay, Amazon.com, or Yahoo.com. This account name and password will serve you throughout the online certification process and will allow you to log in and out as you work on the application.

Rest assured that no one expects you to complete your certification application all in one sitting. However, your application must be completed and submitted within ninety days after you begin the application process online. If your application has not been submitted within that time frame, the entire file will be deleted and you will need to start a new one. You will, however, receive reminder notifications to finish your application during this ninety-day period.

Step 3: Meet your Regional Partner Organization (RPO).

Your online WBENC application will be assigned to a Regional Partner Organization (RPO) for processing. (See appendix A for a full list of RPOs. When you have electronically submitted your application, you will be notified immediately by e-mail with the name of the WBENC regional affiliate that will process your application and your fee for certification. Note that fees may vary from organization to organization and, in some instances, the size of your company.

You will be required to print out your application. (Be certain to keep a copy for your files; it will be useful when you apply for additional certifications from other entities.) You will also need to attach the required documents, such as tax returns, bank signature cards, and proof of citizenship. You will find a comprehensive list of these supporting documents on the website, and you should review it before you begin the application process.

Once you have compiled a complete application package, you must sign an affidavit and have that notarized, then send the notarized affidavit, copy of the application, required documentation, and your check to the organization listed in the e-mail notification.

Take special care to make certain your application is complete when submitted. All RPO leaders agree that missing documents are the single biggest factor in delays in the certification process.

The program managers at each RPO are experts in the certification process. Be sure to access their expertise if you have any questions or problems. These people will also become excellent advisers after you receive your certification, as you navigate the supplier diversity process.

Step 4: Put it all together.

Depending on the size of your business, you may need to contact your accountant and/or lawyer to obtain some of the application documents referenced above. Most sole proprietors and subchapter S corporations find that they have the required documents in their normal business files. The longer you have been in business and the more complicated your business structure (if any of the ownership resides in trusts, for example) the more complicated the application and the process.

Program managers advise WBE applicants to consider their application as a marketing document. "Think about how you want to describe your business and yourself as the CEO; carefully explain exactly what your company does. Check your spelling and grammar before you submit. Do not cut corners! Your application profile will become your online WBE profile when you receive your certification, so you should have a marketing mindset from minute one."

FAQ: What are the biggest mistakes made by certification applicants?

Dr. Marsha Firestone, PhD, president of the Women Presidents' Educational Organization, a WBENC regional partner organization, points out five potential pitfalls:

- **Submitting an incomplete application**—Follow directions! If you neglect to answer all application questions or forget to include required documents, the processing of your application will take extra time.
- **Waiting until the last minute**—There is no way to speed up the certification process, so if a company has requested you become certified in order to do business with them, be sure to give yourself enough time to complete the process. No applications are expedited, no matter what.
- **Not knowing your company's bylaws**—Marsha is often surprised by how many women business owners do not understand their own bylaws. According to Marsha, sometimes the legal documents do not support their claim that they run their company. She says, "They go to an attorney, usually a person who has no experience with certification, and think cookie-cutter bylaws will suffice. They end up creating bylaws that often favor the men in the company. When it comes to certification, this can lead to a denial. Bylaws must state that *all* authority is with the woman, even if this harms some of the male egos in the company."
- **Underpaying yourself**—Not getting paid what you deserve not only hurts your bank account, but it also hurts your WBE certification application. If you own, operate, and control your business, your compensation should

reflect that. The WPEO can cite examples of several businesses where a woman CEO hired her husband to work in the business and paid him more, perhaps to protect his ego or due to questionable financial advice. Nothing raises a red flag faster as to who is *really* running the business than empowering a male business employee. Do not let this happen to you; pay yourself like you are the boss, because you are.

- **Giving up independence**—Many women business owners have a male co-owner or stockholder on whom they rely for advice and information. It is fine to have advisers, but you must fully understand all aspects of your business in order to become certified. As stated in WBENC Standards & Procedures, a WBE cannot have "substantial reliance upon finances and resources of males." If you feel intimidated by issues such as financial statements, take the time to educate yourself now; as your company grows larger, financial management issues will only become more complicated and more important. Do not depend solely on someone else to understand them for you.

Step 5: Review the application.

Approximate time: sixty to ninety days from submission of a complete application.

Once you have submitted your complete application and paid the fee, the staff at the affiliate organization will review your file and contact you if there are missing documents. They may identify special issues that arise in the review of the application and provide a summary to the certification review committee.

An anonymous committee consisting of at least five businesspeople in your region will review your application. They each sign a nondisclosure confidentiality agreement before reviewing your file. The majority of the committee will be composed of representatives from corporations or public entities,

Becoming Certified

and the remainder will be WBEs or representatives of community-based organizations with a related purpose. Most committees include an attorney and a certified public accountant. For WBENC, all committee members undergo detailed, two-day training that is provided remotely by WBENC staff to ensure that the standards are consistently applied throughout the country. Rest assured that competitive businesses are never allowed access to your documentation, review, or discussion.

Note that the committee only makes a recommendation on approval or denial. For WBENC certification, the RPO executive director renders the final decision.

Step 6: Make a site visit.

After the committee has reviewed your complete application, a site visit will be arranged. You must be present at the site visit so that any questions that have arisen during the review process can be answered. In the case of WBENC, the site visit is prescheduled with the woman business owner. The site visit reviewer will ask for clarification on any issues in question from the file review. He or she will ask for an overview of the business and operations in order to get a feel as to how the company operates. He or she will also request a tour of the facilities—but do not worry or clean too much. Certification is not a neatness contest.

Step 7: Find out the results.

You will be notified via e-mail or in writing after your site visit if you are certified *or* denied. When you are approved as a WBE, WBENC provides an explanation of your certification, which includes the description and the North American Industrial Classification System (NAICS) code(s) indicating the functional mission of the business.

Remember that your certification must be renewed annually and site visits are conducted periodically thereafter. You will be notified electronically 120 days prior to your expiration date to provide sufficient time to complete the renewal application. Make certain that your e-mail address is kept up-to-date in the system and that whoever reads your e-mail, if you delegate this process, is aware of the importance of renewing on time. In addition, keep track of your renewal date in your calendar as backup, because recertification is the WBE's responsibility.

OFF AND RUNNING!

When your WBENC partner organization has approved your certification, you will have the privilege of being listed in your certifying organization's database.

While all of the above will take place automatically, certification should act as a starter pistol for you. You should *immediately* begin using your certification as a marketing tool. For openers,

- Add your certification to all your marketing materials, including your business cards, stationery, website, and letterhead. The next chapter provides much more detail about the importance of marketing yourself as a certified business.
- Immediately contact your local WBENC affiliate to start building relationships in the certified community. At this point, you may ask to be matched with a mentor who can help you through the process of marketing yourself to large corporations as a newly certified business.

Once you have determined which companies you would like to target from your earlier research, you must register on each of their supplier diversity websites. According to WBENC's fourteen years of Top Corporations best-practices research, almost all (95 percent) of the corporations with strong supplier diversity programs have a list or database of women and minority enterprise suppliers available to all company buyers.

Becoming Certified

The bad news is that most corporations have their own individual websites, and you will have to register on each and every one of them. This is a good project for your administrative assistant or an intern. Once you have pulled together your information for your WBENC certification application, the data fields for the corporate registrations will be a snap.

I am always surprised when I hear business owners complain about the "burden" of registering on many databases rather than thanking the corporations for the opportunity to register and for their effort to make that registration so accessible. We forget how much more annoying it is to find the right phone number in the company and to have to wait on hold, or to have a call returned and then wait for an application to be mailed. With online registrations, the access is immediate, the accuracy of the information depends on your own input, and there is no middleman to lose or misfile your application.

FAQ: What if my certification is denied?

Some people who apply for WBENC certification do so with the honest belief that they meet the criteria. They describe themselves to friends and relatives as such and believe in their heart of hearts that they are woman business owners. What they do not understand is that "woman-owned business" is not synonymous with "certified Women Business Enterprise (WBE)." They may be a 50/50 partner with a male friend, husband, or other male family member. That does not meet the test. They may hold the largest percent of ownership of a business, but if their ownership along with that of other women owners does not total 51 percent of the voting stock, they do not qualify. Remember, WBENC does not consider community property laws, so joint ownership with a male is not counted.

Denial does not always mean the end of the certification process. Sometimes documents such as bylaws are not clear or actually misstate the control of their company. Listen to Lois Gamerman:

> I found the process of applying for certification with the WBENC relatively easy as opposed to the process I went through to become certified in my home state. The Women's Business Enterprise National Council has a vested interest in and a clearly communicated desire to certify *all* qualifying woman-owned businesses, plain and simple. I was initially denied certification by my home state because I did not complete the voluminous and confusing paperwork properly. I had to go before a state review board as part of the certification process. There were about ten members of the board at the hearing. Only two members asked me any questions; the others read newspapers and balanced checkbooks. By stark contrast, my WBENC representative was approachable, involved, and very helpful.

If your application is denied, the reason for that denial will be included in your notification letter. If the reasons are accurate, you can still market to corporations, just not through the supplier diversity program and not as a certified WBE. If you believe that your documentation has been misinterpreted, contact the partner organization and file an appeal. Your denial may help you develop a good relationship with your local partner organization, as they can coach and counsel you on how to restructure or perhaps reexplain your business to qualify for certification.

CASE STUDY

Rebecca Boenigk, CEO and Chairman of the Board, Neutral Posture, LLC

Rebecca Boenigk has been doing business with the federal government since 1991—long before the creation of WBENC or the WOSB program. Neutral Posture is a leading designer and manufacturer of seating for any and all work environments. I can attest to their products' comfort, as I have one in my home office.

Rebecca and her mom started the company out of the family garage, using a patent for an ergonomic chair obtained by her professor dad. She was certified by WBENC as soon as we were organized and has been a leader working on behalf of her fellow WBEs as chairman of the Women's Enterprise Leadership Forum (The Forum), member of the board, and organizer of the silent auction, whose proceeds help WBENC strengthen programs for certified women-owned businesses.

Rebecca says, "The most meaningful for me personally was my term as chair of The Forum and representing WBEs at the executive committee level on the board. It is a terrific responsibility."

Along with certification, doing business with the government has been a part of the company's marketing strategy since its inception. In just its second year, the company applied for listing on the GSA schedule. This is a contract that can best be compared to a hunting license. "It establishes the terms for me to sell to the government," Rebecca says, "but we have to then market to various agencies and find the business. We have had it since 1991, because we knew it would be important to us. Historically, 20 percent of our business came from this GSA contract."

The contract has nothing to do with being a woman-owned business, because, as Rebecca states, "Most of the buyers still do not get the women business thing." Rebecca believes that there are now opportunities for additional business and hopes that the changes in the WOSB program will create new bidding opportunities. "Originally the contract just covered chairs. We did not have the opportunity to bid on big contracts; we did not even see the bids. Then we discovered that we could add SINs [Special Inventory Numbers detailed on the GSA schedule] and started adding numbers to our existing contract. Specifically, we started looking for what are called 'packaged office contracts.'"

When an agency is seeking a packaged contract, they want a single vendor to supply everything in the office—from the wastebaskets to the cubicles to the desks to the chairs. As a single-item vendor, Neutral Posture did not have a chance until they made the strategic decision that they would team with their competition.

"Once we started getting those bids, our business began to skyrocket. We have already done $1.5 million this year in teaming agreement sales. Doing this is scary for some people. Being president of my industry association has been a huge help, as it has allowed me to pick up the phone and talk to the CEO of the company with which I want to team. I handpicked the companies, called CEOs and said, 'Here is why you should team with us.' They all said yes. My former competitors are now my partners on the teaming agreement."

Rebecca is hopeful that "as the WOSB becomes a bigger player it will help that we have these relationships already established." She also hopes the program will have a "trickle-down impact" on corporations, as many do not separate their WBE spend in their diversity programs.

The National Women's Business Council (NWBC), adviser to the US president, Congress, and the administrator of SBA agrees. Rebecca is a former member of the council, as am I and several other WBENC business owners and RPO leaders. According to its 2011 Annual Report:

> Through the introduction of the Small Business Federal Contract Program, the federal government has helped expand opportunities for women entrepreneurs to secure government contracts with set-asides for only women-owned businesses to compete. The Administration and Congress have made progress in assisting women-owned businesses to compete for and win federal contracts, but more can be done. The SBA Small Business Procurement Scorecard for FY11 shows the

federal government awarded $16.8 billion (3.98%) to companies owned by women, missing its 5% set-aside prime contracting achievement goal for women-owned small business by 1.02%, leaving approximately $4.3 billion in potential contracts for women on the table in FY 11.

Rebecca could be the certification poster child. In addition to her WBE and WOSB certifications, her new Canadian company was recently certified by WEConnect Canada. "We tried to sell into Canada for years, but they are very loyal to Canadian businesses, so we opened a facility outside of Toronto. As required by their laws, we have a Canadian partner. We own 90 percent and are currently doing about $3 million a year."

Chapter Three

Catching the Big Fish: Marketing

Let us deviate from the topic of supplier diversity for a moment and talk about fishing. Yes, fishing. Picture yourself as an ambitious and successful fisherwoman or fisherman, wanting to rise to the next level and catch the fabled "big fish." How would you go about doing this?

First, you would need to obtain a fishing license. Next, you would learn where the big fish live, and when they are in season. Then it would be a good idea to research what the fish like to eat so you can offer the most attractive bait. Finally, you would sit in your home and wait for the fish to swim up to your doorstep.

Huh?

Of course you would not wait for the fish to swim to your doorstep. Most likely you would get up at five in the morning and drive to the exact spot where the fish live, carrying all your equipment and angling expertise with you. You would go back day after day, week after week, learning the patterns and idiosyncrasies of the fish. And eventually, the combination of hard work, knowledge, time, and patience, would result in snaring that big fish.

I use the fishing metaphor because I am constantly surprised at how many women and minority business owners work so hard to acquire a fishing license (certification) and then sit and wait for the big fish (corporate buyers) to come knocking on their doors for business.

Certification is *only a tool*. Becoming certified opens an extraordinary opportunity for your business, but—as I have said before and will no doubt say again—certification does not guarantee that you will win a single corporate contract. Virtually every MWBE and supplier diversity professional I surveyed for this book said that the biggest mistake made by business owners is to assume certification is all they need to win business from corporate America. This could not be more wrong. Certification is like a gym membership—you will not see any benefits unless you use it.

THE ELEVEN COMMANDMENTS OF MWBE MARKETING

Certification must be accompanied by marketing. You need a strategic, multifaceted, long-term marketing plan if you want to do business with the largest companies in America. As a successful business owner, you are likely to be quite familiar with many of the broad concepts in this chapter. Yet I urge you to approach your supplier diversity marketing efforts with a new set of eyes and to remember that you are never done marketing. As the race car driver Mario Andretti once said, "If everything seems under control, you're just not going fast enough."

While you will rely on many of the marketing methods you have already employed to start and grow your business, you will need to alter many of your strategies to compete in the supplier diversity marketplace. The good news is that many MWBEs have ridden this path before you, learning many valuable lessons that can make your path easier. Their wisdom—and warnings—appear throughout this chapter's list of eleven "marketing commandments" for doing business through the supplier diversity door to opportunity.

WBENC frequently hears that the top challenge to successfully selling large corporations cited by women was *learning about opportunities*. The good news is that you can take steps to maximize your chances of learning about opportunities. As the first commandment on market research will demonstrate, you need to be proactive about researching opportunities through the Internet, associations, supplier diversity contacts, and your WBE colleagues and competitors. Knowledge truly is power, and you need to have it in spades to succeed as a supplier to corporate America. Remember that in today's world, you have to add social networking to your strategy—both to spread information about your business and to learn more about your target corporation.

FIRST COMMANDMENT: KNOW THY MARKET

There is only one place to start your strategic marketing planning: market research about potential customers. You must learn as much as you possibly can about your new corporate customer base. Many newly certified businesses have made the mistake of targeting their marketing efforts to corporations that do not even purchase what they produce or the service they provide.

One of the advantages of contacting a corporate supplier diversity department is the large amount of information you can gather about your corporate customers. There is absolutely no excuse for ignorance. Besides the company's own website and publications, you can find an enormous amount of information in major newspapers, magazines, and trade association publications. Supplier diversity contacts can provide additional insight and help you to target your approach within their companies.

You should never contact a company without knowing as much as you can about what they purchase, when they purchase it, how they like to be contacted, and who the key players are. In our highly networked world, there is simply no excuse for lack of knowledge about a company.

How important is research? Let me count the ways.

A variety of supplier diversity experts from diverse companies weigh in on the importance of researching your potential corporate customers:

Catching the Big Fish: Marketing

"It's vital," says Marianne Strobel of AT&T. "I look for WBEs that bring timely and creative solutions to AT&T. When WBEs research our company's initiatives, strategies, industry trends, and customer offerings, they are better prepared to have a solid value proposition. I can tell when a WBE has done their homework and it signals they are serious about winning our business. It also indicates that they are likely to be a top-performing company in their industry. A WBE must research my company to understand what we do and where our company is heading to help us with that mission."

"Thoroughly researching your customer and their market is paramount to gaining a finely honed competitive edge," says Maria Guerrero, vice president of Marketing & Strategic Relationships, the DW Morgan Company, Inc.

"When we engage a WBE to work on our behalf, we only do so when we *know* they have put in the necessary work to understand our challenges and opportunities. By thoroughly understanding our company and our market, a WBE is then prepared to collaboratively work with us and become a trusted partner in making the right choices for our business. Well-prepared WBEs have been integral to the health, wealth, and growth of our company."

Below is a checklist of what you need to know about every corporate customer you plan to target with your marketing efforts. The more you know about your potential customers, the more you will be able to craft your marketing messages to address their desires and concerns—and the better you can avoid companies that are unlikely to work with you. Conduct this research for every corporation on your prospect list.

What do they purchase? This is the most basic information you need to know. Good supplier diversity websites, such as the UPS site featured in appendix D, include a full list of their purchasing needs. Lists like UPS's do not serve as a guarantee that a company will purchase any of the listed products from a WBE, but they provide guidance to suppliers about what products or services they will even consider procuring.

FAQ: What if my product or service is too unique to appear on a purchasing list, but I believe the corporation would be interested in what I provide?

This is where a visit to a national business fair, such as those sponsored by WBENC and our partner organizations, is a good investment. Most major corporations will have representatives present with whom you can chat, either on the fair floor or at the many networking sessions and content workshops that take place in conjunction with these events. Putting a face with a name will provide an enhanced opportunity for in-person, telephone, or e-mail communication. (See chapter four for more information on business and trade fairs.)

If appropriate, you might also send a product sample and ask for a critique from a supplier diversity executive with whom you have a good relationship. One WBE built a prototype instrument (at her own expense) to demonstrate that her company could handle a highly technical piece of business. She reviewed it with her customer, Johnson & Johnson. This extra effort impressed the buyers and won the WBE an even larger contract than she had before.

Here is how Lois Gamerman uses her unique advantage: "We are the only WBENC-certified food service distributor operating in this region. Usually large corporate feeders purchase their products from the Syscos and USFoods of the world. When I created this company twenty-three years ago, it was important to me to define our product offerings as products that could not be purchased through large, broad-line foodservice distributors. Setting ourselves apart from the competition meant that we could not only bring new and diverse products to market, but we could also give them the added bonus of increasing their spending with a diversity supplier."

Just one example of the payoff of her strategy is this story with a happy ending: "Soft Stuff Distributors approached Avendra, the purchasing arm of Marriott and Hyatt, to become an approved supplier dozens of times over several years. Every attempt was met with frustration with trying to navigate the system. Finally, after a wonderful meeting with Tom Villenue, director of Regional Procurement Northeast, we found ourselves in the position to realize our goal of signing a contract to provide products to their hotel properties. Our persistence paid off, because after my first meeting with Tom, we received the very great news that day that they approved us as the diversity partner for ice cream distribution. Seven years later we are still servicing their properties, and our business with Avendra is growing."

FAQ: *When do they purchase?*

Rondu Vincent, manager of supplier diversity at Pfizer, says he hears the "when" question frequently. This information appears on the Pfizer website (as it does on most supplier diversity sites), but Rondu says it is actually the wrong question to ask. "Remember, we do not have opportunities every day," he says, "and if we do have opportunities, we often already have a preferred supplier in mind. So the better question is, what can you do to market yourself internally at a company to find out about opportunities when they do arise and to become a preferred supplier yourself?"

In addition to heeding Rondu's wise advice, remember that, in general, corporate purchasing may not take place according to the schedule or quantity allotment you may be accustomed to with smaller customers. In fact, a retail store like Macy's may purchase Christmas stock nine to twelve months in advance. Be sure to include timing in your company research, as it will become important later when you think about matching your production and distribution processes to your corporate customers' timetables.

FAQ: How much do they purchase?

What is the average dollar amount spent on purchases in your niche? Is your point-of-sale price higher or lower than that of the company's existing suppliers? What is each company's current usage of your type of product or service offering, and is that usage likely to increase or decrease? How much do they buy at a time?

FAQ: What department is responsible for purchasing your product or service?

While the supplier diversity department will be your entry point, it is important to learn as much as possible about the actual division(s) of the corporation that will make the final decision about your product. Your supplier diversity contacts will help lead you through the corporate maze, but even they may not know about *all* potential opportunities for your products or services. Be creative, resourceful, and patient; diligently research the companies you are targeting, and listen to what they tell you about their business needs across the corporation.

According to Brian Hall, supplier diversity and outreach specialist and small-business liaison officer for Shell: "The first question I often ask a WBE is 'Do you have any relationships outside the diversity or procurement office?' I find that the most successful WBEs are very strategic in their approach. They exhibit patience as they learn about where our company/industry is headed, how the company works, and its processes and people, culture, and values. A key to all of this is how successful the WBE is at developing relationships outside the procurement organization, in particular the business units. Only then can the WBE truly uncover and understand the needs of the company and work to apply a solution."

Catching the Big Fish: Marketing

While you are thinking creatively about where you might fit into a corporation, it is also OK to think small. After all, the small fish can often lead you to the bigger catches, as Julia Rhodes of KleenSlate attests.

SUCCESS STORY

JULIA RHODES, PRESIDENT AND CEO, KLEENSLATE CONCEPTS

While I have updated and replaced most of the stories in this book, I just had to include this one from WBENC's earliest days. When we first met Julia, she had a single product: a dry-erase marker and eraser for white boards. KleenSlate now produces a number of creative products and services diverse industries from schools to office supplies to hospitals to Hollywood.

Let's start at the beginning. It is both funny and interesting how necessity, lack of resources, and a good imagination can be combined to create a simple yet successful marketing tool. In 2001, after inventing and receiving her patent for the Kleenslate Attachable Eraser for dry-erase markers, Julia was preparing to launch the eraser at her first WBENC National Conference and Business Fair show. She realized that, because she would be working the event alone, her presentation had to be simple. Both of her hands would already be busy, holding the dry-erase markers and showing the Kleenslate Eraser in action.

Coincidentally, Julia was also trying to decide what to wear to the trade show, and a light bulb appeared: Could she create an outfit was a walking whiteboard? Online research yielded a peel-and-stick whiteboard product that she could apply to the little black dresses left over from her days as a jazz singer. She called on the creativity of a friend, and together they altered the dresses to create wearable whiteboard surfaces. The large, circular dots of peel-and-stick whiteboard gave her dresses an eye-catching, 1960s "mod" look. Add a pair of white go-go boots, and people could not help but notice Julia and her product.

Wearing the Kleenslate outfit freed her hands and enabled her to write on herself and then easily erase with the Kleenslate Eraser while providing an instantly memorable impression. When Julia demonstrated her Kleenslate products at trade shows and conventions, she often got the reaction, "Can I write on you?" or "What a great party idea!" or "Aha! I wondered why you were dressed like that!"

Julia is happy for any approach that initiates conversation and allows her to talk about her product. When she pursues her potential clients after shows, she always receives instant recognition as well as a friendly reception when she identifies herself as "the whiteboard eraser gal."

This creative marketing tactic helped Julia succeed with corporate clients in particular. At a WBENC business fair, she met Robert McCormes-Ballou, then director of vendor diversity for Office Depot. Intrigued by the product, Robert connected Julia with his assistant, Shari Francis, to further advance the relationship. Shari and Julia then developed a working relationship, which ultimately led to an Office Depot ad featuring Kleenslate.

As Julia says, "The door had opened, and I stepped on through." Now you can find Kleenslate Erasers at all 850 Office Depot retail stores. Julia says, "Office Depot continues to walk the walk. They even have a special catalog for their diverse suppliers. I get thirty to forty orders a day from them and drop ship all over the country,"

Today you can find Julia's products at Office Depot as well as at Kleenslate.com and other office supply stores. A Staples representative saw Julia's products in the Office Depot booth at a WBENC business fair, and they too are now a customer. Julia Rhodes certainly caught the big fish!

Catching the Big Fish: Marketing

A former schoolteacher, Julia also developed a dry-erase paddle for classroom use ("I call it a high-touch product in a high-tech world") that was recently featured on a *Today Show* "Back to School" episode. The paddle has been used by Anderson Cooper to get audience feedback for his new daytime show and has been adapted for hospital use in patient communication. KleenSlate was featured on the Jay Leno Show in an "Invent across America" segment.

Julia's entertainment industry connection even goes to Hollywood itself. A summer job in Santa Fe working for a company that produced commercials and music videos led to a new outlet for her dry erasers. Julia remembered that they would tape powder puffs to markers to erase those "take two" slates. When she sent a sample to a company called Film Tools, they demanded that she overnight 1,250 for the next day. That business grew into markers and a whole line of products specifically for the industry.

According to Julia, "It is impossible to really measure just how important a role that little whiteboard outfit played in the whole scheme of things, but I have absolutely no doubt it didn't hurt."

Think about how you might "start small" with some of your target prospects, perhaps offering a limited range of products or services, or serving a specific geographic area. Who knows, like Julia, it may lead not only to new corporate customers but also to whole new industries.

FAQ: How do they purchase?

Become an expert in the administrative practices of your prospect companies. Does the company procure entirely online? Do they demand many face-to-face meetings? Do they require you to warehouse the product under contract and deliver "just in time"? If so, what are the additional costs to your company and what are the increased risks? You will want to think about including your ability to meet certain administrative or technological requirements in your marketing materials (see chapter six for more information on technology).

FAQ: How is the company positioned now and into the future?

Pay close attention to industry trends related to the future of your products or services, as well as the future of the companies with which you would like to do business. Are there any timely, urgent issues you can address? Are there any major technological changes down the road that you can anticipate? (Think of all the typewriter suppliers who lost business when computers took over.) Are there rumors of mergers or acquisitions among particular companies? How are the company's finances? One successful WBE admits that, early on, she made the mistake of supplying companies that were near bankruptcy, because she did not research their ability to pay. This resulted in some bad debt for her.

Senior procurement executives recommend that you research the company's

- goals and objectives,
- mission statement and business model,
- industry challenges—is the industry growing, on a plateau or in decline?—and
- major competitors.

Are they currently gaining or losing market share, and why? Remember, however, that any of the above information you discover does not prevent you from marketing to a particular company (in fact, some changes can be advantageous to suppliers), but should be part of your due diligence when creating a marketing strategy. As we will explore throughout this book, your job as a marketer is to tie *your* value proposition to the corporation's specific mission and goals. The most compelling sales pitches explain how *you* can solve a corporation's business challenges.

They also point out that corporate business models and their associated goals, challenges, and supplier opportunities are always subject to change. For example, many IT and telecom OEM (original equipment manufacturer) companies that used to be in the business of manufacturing are now completely outsourcing the manufacturing and warehousing of their products to focus exclusively on the research and development of new product offerings. A dozen years ago, this was unthinkable, but these industries' business models have shifted. This creates a vast opening for MWBEs in the IT manufacturing sector. Can you benefit from a shift in the way corporations in your industry do business? Keep your finger on the pulse of your field to detect potential changes and opportunities.

In their handbook *I'm Certified, Now What?* Carol Dougal and Hedy Ratner of the Women's Business Development Center in Chicago remind certified businesses not to consider *all* corporations as their target market. You will be required to invest serious time and energy in following up with every corporation you contact by filling out vendor application forms and/or making follow-up phone calls. Consider whether you have the staff to build relationships with hundreds of corporations. Be realistic.

SECOND COMMANDMENT: KNOW THY COMPETITION

To make your marketing message stand out to a corporate supplier diversity representative, you need to differentiate yourself from the crowd—a.k.a. your competitors.

You will want to find out the following:

Who are my primary competitors, and are they doing business with any of the companies I plan to market to?

Breaking Through

The Internet has changed everything, and *Google* has become a verb. But there are many ways to find an answer to this question in varying degrees of industry-specific sophistication. Networking in trade associations can provide information. Industry newsletters sometimes include information on recently completed agreements. If your target company is a government contractor, they are required to list the names of their diverse subcontractors in their subcontracting plans. If the company is retail, you can visit a location to determine what they are buying and from whom and how it is displayed. Do not forget the most obvious method: ask the buyer, who will often tell you directly.

Do your research on all competitors, whether or not they are MWBEs, as you will likely be competing with both. And even if you are a small shop, learn who the big players are in your industry. You may want to borrow their tactics or connect with their leaders for advice, mentoring, or strategic alliances. Do not forget that there may be second-tier opportunities for you with a prime contractor. (See chapter five for information about strategic alliances and second-tier supplying opportunities.)

What are the strengths and weaknesses of my competitors?

Do your best to collect competitors' ads and literature. Study them for information about strategy, product features, and benefits. At the very least, familiarize yourself with the website of each competitor. When you are redesigning any of your marketing materials, look to your competitor file for ways to differentiate yourself. Ask, what opportunities can I find in the weaknesses of my competitors? Am I faster? Less expensive? More technologically advanced?

When I was a manufacturers' representative, I would visit a retail outlet of each of the companies I called on before I made that first call. As I was already familiar with my competition from attending semi-annual trade shows, I could tell on the spot who they were buying from, the apparent age of the merchandise (which told me whether it was appropriate for their market or priced correctly), the pricing and mark-down policies, and the general tastes of the buyer. That information allowed me to hone my pitch and close more business.

Competitive research needs to be part of your ongoing marketing strategy, even when you secure and begin to service corporate contracts. The supplier diversity marketplace, as is true of the entire business marketplace, is very competitive, and you need to stay one step ahead of the game.

Once you have done your research on what your corporate customers need and what your competitors are lacking, it is time to show how your company is the perfect solution.

Third Commandment: Know Thyself

All of your marketing messages should include information about your company's unique value proposition in the overall marketplace—and in the MWBE marketplace in particular. What will make you stand out to a supplier diversity representative or purchasing manager? Remember, with corporate customers, it is just as important to market your capacity to do business with the big guys as it is to market your products or services.

Eyvon C. Austin, the global director of supplier diversity at the Coca-Cola Company, provides this insight from the corporation's perspective:

> Diversity in business yields innovation, greater productivity, and a competitive advantage in the marketplace. In that regard, WBEs must be prepared by researching the goals and objectives, industry challenges, and other areas of concern of targeted companies. They must focus on the products and services they can provide and recognize their strengths and limitations by not promising what they cannot deliver. Moreover, they must recognize that it is more productive to focus on opportunities and companies with which they will

have a higher probability of success and reach out to the supplier diversity office for coaching and to serve as an advocate as they pursue opportunities with the targeted companies.

Successful WBE Rosalie Edson agrees: "It is my personal commitment and our corporate philosophy at Meadows to never be satisfied with our efforts, but always to strive for higher levels of proficiency and professionalism. Outstanding customer service is delivered by people who work from the heart. Every day we grow, we expand our knowledge base, and we learn."

Cheat Sheet

Consider these questions when defining your value proposition and developing marketing messages that will appeal to the companies you plan to approach:

Defining Your Value Proposition

- Do you have a highly specialized product or service that few companies offer?

- Can you offer a smaller or cheaper version of a particular product or service?

- Can you offer a fancier or more expensive version of a particular product or service?

- Do you offer a higher level of experience than your competitors?

- Are you geographically desirable?

- Do you have strong technological and

administrative capabilities that prove your ability to work efficiently with a large corporate buyer?

- Are you more creative than your competitors?

- Are you faster than your competitors?

- Are you more cost-effective than your competitors?

- Are you more flexible in terms of design modifications?

- Do you offer a broader catalog of synergistic products?

- Does your financing structure offer greater flexibility in payment terms?

- Do you have compatible technologies?

- Are you registered with electronic commerce entities utilized by the client?

- Are you "green"?

JuriSolutions has used their size to prove that they are nimble in providing new billing models. They scrapped the traditional legal hourly billing model and introduced a system that bills according to gigabyte of data. Attorney Cindy Tower says, "We used to conduct document review by searching through files provided in cardboard boxes. There was no predictable way to determine how long it would take to get through each box. Today data is provided electronically, and we were able to come up with a system that is able to predict how long it takes to review a gigabyte of data. This provides a measurable outcome for our clients."

If you are a small business, be sure to promote the positive aspects of large corporations' doing business with you. Many companies value and leverage the unique values that small businesses provide, such as responsiveness, creativity, innovation, flexibility, service, customization, and quality. While you might face challenges as a small business, you can do everything in your power to create the positive marketing messages that point out the strengths of your size.

Fourth Commandment: Create New Collateral around Thy Certification

If you have it, flaunt it! No one will know you are a certified business unless you share the news. Upon receiving your certification, add the logo of the certifying organization to your e-mail signature, business cards, website, letterhead, trade-show booth, and all other marketing materials. This seal of approval will be noticed by purchasers, competitors, and potential networking contacts—and will work to your advantage. In addition to including your certification in marketing materials, I recommend including any industry or association affiliations as well. They all promote your credibility as a company poised to do business in major markets. If you have other certifications, such as ISO 9000, prominently list those as well.

Will these changes and new materials cost money? Some will; some won't. But you really do have to spend money to make money. Changing your e-mail signature costs nothing. When updating your website, there are a vast array of solutions from do-it-yourself to very sophisticated. Remember, when you plan to do business with large, successful corporations, you will need to look the part. If you are unhappy with your current image, certification can act as an opportunity to update your

Catching the Big Fish: Marketing

company's look. But do not tinker too much with what has worked to make your business successful to this point. Creating certification-related marketing messages and materials should *complement* your existing image and branding, not necessarily replace it.

The biggest single change in the world of marketing and communications since writing the last edition of this book is the rise of social media. According to Susie Aubuchon, a consultant with McKinley Marketing Partners,

> They [WBEs] need a certain mind-set. There has been a paradigm shift on communication model. Even the "paid" model has been heavily influenced by social media. You have no control over the world's view of your brand unless you set the agenda. Instead of paid media, the emphasis is on "earned media"—the information about you or your company that goes viral. You cannot get earned media unless you have a platform. In addition to your website, you need to be on LinkedIn, Facebook, Instagram, Pinterest, and Twitter. That is where your customers are creating the value of your brand, because they have a say in it.

Be certain to update your LinkedIn and Facebook profiles, and you should tweet about your certification when it is new or renewed. If you attend a supplier diversity event, whether sponsored by WBENC, a corporation, or your RPO, take a video with your phone or tablet, and post that as well.

Collateral materials are enormously important. As we all know, first impressions are crucial. Here are some additional tips gathered from WBENC-certified businesses:

- Put your certification front and center. This is a great tip for any certified business, but can be particularly helpful for young companies. Ask certified businesses for recommendations of graphic artists, copywriters, web designers, and other marketing professionals who can provide expert services. This is not the time for you to experiment with clip art. Whenever possible, you may want to give your business to a fellow WBE and perhaps barter your services. If you are WBENC-certified yourself, you can search WBENCLink, the Internet-accessible database of WBE firms.

- Produce separate business cards and marketing literature for each of your target market segments if they require different messages. For instance, you might want to create separate brochures for government and corporate clients or for business-to-business and business-to-consumer audiences.

- Consider purchasing a memorable domain name or toll-free phone number that relates to your business so your prospects can easily contact you. Could anyone forget Ukrainian egg artist, author, and professional speaker Jane Pollak's 877-EGG-LADY?

- Create low-cost focus groups. Test your new marketing materials on friends, staff members, and other business people, particularly corporate executives. Do they feel your logo appears professional enough? Is your website clear and easy to navigate? Are there any mistakes or inconsistencies in your marketing pieces? Do not let a prospect be the first to alert you to a typo in the brochure of which you just printed ten thousand copies.

FIFTH COMMANDMENT: TAKE FULL ADVANTAGE OF THY ONLINE MARKETING OPPORTUNITIES

As you have no doubt noticed, much of the business of supplier diversity takes place online: company research, certification, database listings, and more. This means a large proportion of your marketing efforts should also take place on the web.

Catching the Big Fish: Marketing

Now that you are certified, you have the privilege of listing your business on many websites, databases, and directories for purchasers. Take advantage of every easy opportunity to market your business. One caveat: be sure to proofread your directory listings and keep them updated with any changes in contact information, product offerings, or other news. Do not let your listings become stale. Keep a record of all your postings for easy management.

In addition to the previously discussed acts of listing your certified business with WBENC and your local partner organization and the corporations with which you would like to do business, list your business with the following:

- Local chambers of commerce
- Industry trade associations
- The US government's Central Contractor Registration, which is now SAM. There has recently been a mass migration of all 650,000 CCR registrations and ORCA certifications into an entirely new data system called SAM (System for Award Management). All new registrations and mandatory annual revalidations must now be completed in this new SAM System. If an organization already had a registration in the old CCR system (now referred to as Legacy Accounts), they must now be updated and reestablished into the new system following the new procedures and guidelines put in place.

Create the highest-quality website you can afford.

Many supplier diversity professionals and purchasing managers will visit your website as part of the vetting process. Make sure that your site accurately reflects your brand, your competitive edge, and your capacity to do business with large customers. If you are still living with a website your teenager designed in the

Breaking Through

early days of the Internet (you know who you are!), now is definitely the time to upgrade.

Here are additional suggestions from the most web-savvy MWBEs I know:

- If you have not already done so, obtain a memorable URL that is as close as possible to your business name. Be sure to acquire e-mail addresses with this URL as well. It is much more impressive and not expensive at all to have an e-mail address of "Jane@JaneDoeEnterprises.com" than JaneDoeEnterprises@hotmail.com. It is amazing to me that I still get e-mails from entrepreneurs with gmail extensions.
- On the topic of e-mail, create a "signature" to appear at the bottom of all e-mail messages you send. This signature should include your full contact information, website URL (including an active link to click to your website) and, of course, your certification. Online marketing experts also recommend adding a customized line at the bottom of your signature: the tagline of your company, information about an upcoming event at which you are speaking, a new product launch, or the name of a book or article you have recently written. On my own business signature, I include the tag line: "Oh, by the way, I am never too busy for your referrals."
- Do not be shy about using your e-mail signature to announce awards you have won (see the next section for advice on applying for awards) or honors you have received. I recently promoted my book *The Guide to Moving Mom*, including a link to the online bookstore where it can be purchased.
- Mention your website address (URL) on *all* your marketing materials—no exceptions! And ask everyone to "friend" you on Facebook. Build you network.
- Make sure that all your contact information is available and easy to find on your website, preferably on a standard

"Contact Us" page. Do not make a prospective buyer search for a way to call you if he or she wants to meet you! Regularly google yourself and your company to see how your name comes up in searches for your product, service, or company. If it is not coming up the way you believe it should, talk to your website designer about maximizing your search engine results.

- Include all recent press releases, news articles, bylined articles, and other proof that you are on the move and recognized in your industry or community. Do not be shy about promoting any publicity you have received. No press release? Why not? Take every opportunity to write a press release. The word *press* is loosely used. You can send the release to local business journals and industry papers, or just post on LinkedIn or Facebook. But do not forget to send it to your customers and prospects as well. See some samples at the end of this section.
- Create an area of your website specifically for customer and potential customers. This area can provide tailored content so your valued clients can immediately find the information that is relevant to their needs. Do not make your clients surf around your site to find the information they need.
- Include downloadable information documents on your site (such as that press release you just created), preferably in PDF format. This will allow prospective customers and others to read any position papers, annual reports, or other documents that may be too long or text-heavy to include as web pages. This can be a particularly good strategy for owners of companies that produce complicated products. Even if your product or service is not complicated, you should always have your graphic-design firm provide you with PDF versions of any new brochures or reports. PDFs are good for two reasons: most people have the software (Adobe Acrobat) to open the files, and PDF files cannot be altered when downloaded from your website (as Word or PowerPoint files can).

- Update your site frequently (at least once a month) with "news flashes" on the homepage, new client listings, new testimonials, or other fresh content. No one returns to a site that seems stagnant or neglected. Be certain to mention if you are a speaker or a panelist for a business conference or community event. Robyn Streisand, the CEO of THE MIXX, advises, "Provide a link on your website to a LinkedIn page for your company. This will in turn allow people to see members of your team and also give potential customers other points of contact and outreach."

Cheat Sheet

Sample Press Releases
Oculus, Inc., Nationally Recertified

(St. Louis—November 6, 2012)—Oculus, Inc., a business specializing in architecture, strategic planning, interior design, and move management, received national recertification as a Women's Business Enterprise by the Women's Business Development Center, Chicago, a regional certifying partner of the Women's Business Enterprise National Council.

The Women's Business Enterprise National Council's national standard of certification implemented by the Women's Business Development Center, Chicago, is a meticulous process including an in-depth review of the business and site inspection. The certification process is designed to confirm the business is at least 51 percent owned, operated, and controlled by a woman or women.

By including women-owned businesses among their suppliers and corporations, government agencies demonstrate their commitment to fostering diversity and the continued development of their supplier/vendor diversity programs.

Catching the Big Fish: Marketing

About Oculus, Inc.

Oculus, Inc., is a national, WBE-certified, full-service architecture and consulting services firm with offices in St. Louis and Dallas. We help our clients thrive in today's fast-paced world by providing Architectural Design, Interior Design, Strategic Facility Planning, and Move Management Services. We work closely with our clients to achieve maximum value for their facilities and real-estate investments. For information on Oculus, Inc., please call (314) 367-6100, or visit www.oculusinc.com.

About WBENC

The Women's Business Enterprise National Council is the nation's largest third-party certifier of businesses owned, operated, and controlled by women in the United States. WBENC is a resource for the more than 700 US companies and government agencies that rely on WBENC's certification as an integral part of their supplier diversity programs.

* * * * *

Shepherd Data Services (R) Named a Certified Women's Business Enterprise

Full-Service Litigation Support Company Achieves Recognition from the Women's Business Enterprise National Council

(MINNEAPOLIS—(Marketwire)—11/14/12) Shepherd Data Services (Shepherd), a Minneapolis-based leader in full-service litigation support, including e-discovery and review technology, today announced it has been recognized by the Women's Business Enterprise National Council (WBENC) as a certified Women's Business Enterprise.

Founded in 2002 by Christine Chalstrom, president and CEO of

Breaking Through

Shepherd, the 100 percent woman-owned business has grown from a one-person operation to a full-service professional firm of legal, technology, IT, software, and project management experts. Shepherd has expanded its portfolio of services, which has yielded incredible growth despite economic challenges. From its high-volume data processing to its cutting-edge portfolio of licensed legal software, the company has become a leading litigation support company in the Twin Cities.

"I am proud to be a leader in the legal technology industry and thankful to our clients and business partners for contributing to our success," said Chalstrom. "I look forward to Shepherd's future and hope that our certification as a WBE-owned business will lead to additional partnerships and new opportunities to build on that success."

Certifying women-owned businesses are the foundation of the WBENC's mission. WBENC certification validates that the business is 51 percent owned, operated, and controlled by a woman or women. To achieve WBENC certification, women-owned businesses complete a formal documentation and site visit process administered by one of WBENC's fourteen regional partner organizations. WBENC certification gives women-owned businesses the ability to compete for real-time business opportunities provided by WBENC corporate members and government agencies. WBENC certification is accepted by more than a thousand corporations representing America's most prestigious brands, in addition to many states, cities, and other entities.

About Shepherd Data Services:

Shepherd Data Services (Shepherd) is not just a vendor—it is part of a litigation team. With more than ten years of service to the litigation community, Shepherd provides unsurpassed professional services, guidance, expertise, cutting-edge processes, and trial support. The company offers out-of-the-box thinking, individualized and personalized attention, and advice for every aspect of the case. Shepherd meets the demands of the legal marketplace through high-quality and process-efficient production standards. Shepherd combines experience in the legal industry and a thorough knowledge of programming and litigation support software programs to deliver unparalleled service for large and small cases alike. To learn more, please visit www.shepherddata.com.

Press Contact:
Bridget A. Sullivan
Shepherd Data Services
(612) 659-1234

SIXTH COMMANDMENT: MARKET THYSELF AS AN EXPERT

Corporate purchasers are interested in the specifics of your business, but they are also very interested in you as the owner and operator of your business. Take advantage of opportunities to market yourself as the head of your company and as an industry leader. Some women, especially those of us "of a mature age," do not want to appear pushy (or we learned at a young age that "the boys will not like it"), so we do not put ourselves up front. This is a mistake. You absolutely can be present and polite at the same time. In fact, the success of your business may depend on your ability to politely and professionally promote yourself as a business owner.

Create marketing materials about you.

Pay as much attention to the writing and editing of your professional bio as you do to the marketing copy promoting your business. Post your bio on your website and include it in marketing packages for potential customers. A professional, up-to-date headshot is essential as well. (While digital cameras are terrific to document the company picnic, rely on a professional to create your headshot.)

Speak at professional events.

Professional speaking is a great way to make yourself known in your industry. Contact your local RPO, industry association, chamber of commerce, Rotary Club, or other organization (see "Resource Guide" in appendix C for additional suggestions) to learn about opportunities to speak about important issues in your field or your local business community.

If you do not have the time or the desire to prepare a keynote address, seek out opportunities to speak on panels instead. Another option for the time-pressed (or nervous) is to speak virtually. Many organizations and businesses now host webinars, some featuring live chats with speakers.

Cheat Sheet

Speak Up! Making the Most of Your Public Speaking

When you do speak, virtually or in-person, maximize the experience.

- Invite business partners, clients, potential customers, supplier diversity contacts, and the press to attend your events. Although they may not come, people will certainly make note of your status as a professional expert.

- On your website, promote the events at which you are speaking.

- Ask someone to take photographs during your

speech (digital, if possible). You can post these on your website or include them in press kits to show your expert status.

- Make sure you are presented the way you want to be. Bring your own bio to provide to the person who will introduce you.

- Discuss your certification in your remarks to show your credibility and increase your appeal to any potential corporate customers in the audience.

- Videotape your speeches so you can review your performance at a later date and can add it to your YouTube channel. This is easy to do with the technology on many phones and tablets. If you cannot video your speech, audiotape yourself with a small, handheld recorder or right from your iPad.

- Bring plenty of business cards and other marketing materials to any event at which you speak. Leave your cards on a table or hand them to all attendees. I sometimes bring copies of my most recent book; it offers value, contains contact information, and is memorable.

- Try to obtain a list of attendees at any speaking engagement so you can follow up with potential leads, or add attendees to your marketing database.

Write articles or blog posts.

There are hundreds of opportunities to write and publish expert articles. If you can't get placement in an industry journal, search out blogs that would welcome your input, or start your own. I subscribe to www.HARO.com. HARO stands for "Help a Reporter Out." Through their daily e-mails, I have had opportunities to be interviewed for radio talk shows as well as provide blog posts and quotes for articles.

You can pitch articles as short as five hundred words to an industry association newsletter, e-newsletter, website, magazine, or other publication. Consider the business section of your local newspaper as well. At the very least, publish your articles on your own company's website and share the link on Facebook. A bylined article is a great indicator not only of your expert status, but also of your desire to share your views with other professionals in your field. Make high-quality copies, and bring them to your speaking engagements.

To maximize the marketing potential of your written pieces, do the following:

- Always send a thank-you note to the editor who hired you to write for the publication. Keep these relationships strong so editors will keep your name on file and invite you to write more articles in the future. While e-mail works well for most people, it does not have the impact of a handwritten and mailed note.
- Post your written articles on your website and include reprints in any media kits or other marketing packages. WBE Nancy Michaels, president of GrowYourBusiness.com, suggests that you reprint any published articles in color (if the original article appeared that way) and on the highest quality paper stock available; no one is impressed by smudged photocopies.

- Cross market by writing a press release (and posting it prominently on your website) directing people to the article source. For basically the same amount of work, you get double exposure. That way, if your clients or prospects do not have time to read the article, they will at least get a pithy quote or key message digested in the press release.

Apply for awards.

Awards are important credentials that can help your marketing efforts. The next chapter offers advice on applying for awards given by associations to which you belong. WBENC and its partner organizations have awards programs, as do most local certification bodies. For example, Roz Lewis, executive director of the Greater Women's Business Council says, "Each year we honor and recognize our top corporations at our Top Corporations luncheon. This event is held in the spring. In the fall, we host our annual LACE (Ladies Achieving Continuous Excellence) event, where we honor and celebrate our winners, who are Advocate of the Year, Corporation of the Year, Buyer of the Year, Trailblazer of the Year, and Volunteer of the Year. The Voice Award is a corporate award selected by the WBE selection committee."

Additional places to look for award opportunities include chambers of commerce, volunteer organizations, local and national newspapers and magazines, and university alumni associations. When you do win an award, be sure to send a press release to the media and your existing and potential customers to share the good news. If you have to buy a table at the awards dinner, invite your supplier diversity contact as your guest. Also add awards to your professional bio and, of course, your website. This is a good way to get a free professional press release. I stay in touch with the editor of my business school's magazine, and she has written two press releases in the past year about me. The first announced my book *The Guide to Moving Mom* and the second announced a seminar I am presenting on campus.

Patty Klein from A-Plus Meetings & Incentives applied for and was a winner of Ernst & Young's Winning Women Award in 2011. According to Patty, "It has been terrific. It enabled me to attend the Strategic Growth Forums in 2011 and 2012 and attend sessions where Ernst & Young provided excellent training and coaching on how the winners can grow their businesses."

At the Strategic Growth Forums, which are focused on entrepreneurial growth, there are opportunities to network with financiers, entrepreneurs, and Fortune 500 leaders. "I have generated leads from these and am still working the network," Patty says. "The E&Y training and willingness to help the Winning Women in any way is outstanding, and I will continue to tap into their connections for additional leads."

Conduct and promote original research.

Particularly if you produce a very unique product or service, conduct surveys and research projects to educate your customers about your specialty. To gather information, marketing expert Joyce L. Bosc recommends including a postage-paid survey card with your brochures and other company literature that asks customers and potential customers for feedback that can help you develop relevant products and services. Survey Monkey is an easy-to-use tool that allows you to conduct frequent surveys and even change them for target markets. Constant Contact, which I use to distribute my monthly e-newsletters, now has a survey tool. The best thing about this is that I already have my 1,600 contact e-mails in the system and have them divided into appropriate e-lists. With these tools, anyone can produce a professional survey.

You can also offer a coupon, discount, or other reward for survey participants. Once you have your research findings, develop a press release or article to announce your results to your customers, potential customers, the media, and other relevant audiences in your industry. You might also incorporate targeted survey results into a new business pitch.

Many major news outlets are hungry for data-driven interview topics. This is especially true around major events. The Women Presidents' Organization, for example, surveys its members on employment issues and announces the results as a "Labor Day" survey.

Be an industry resource.

Another smart way to demonstrate your expertise and stay top-of-mind with potential customers is to forward news articles and items of interest to your supplier diversity contacts. Writing "I thought this might interest you…" at the top of a forwarded industry article you have read is a great way to keep in touch without being a pest. This type of simple, no-cost marketing technique is great for managing the long months of the corporate decision-making process.

My stockbroker is really good at this, and hardly a day goes by without a PDF of an interesting article about a stock I already own or one she believes I might be interested in. The subject line of the e-mail is clear, so I can decide instantaneously whether to read, delete, or save. This method of communication is fast and inexpensive.

If you set up "blast" lists that you want to send materials to, be certain to put the list in the "bcc" (blind carbon copy) line of the address so that each recipient sees only his or her own name and not the entire list. Or, even better, use a distribution system such as Constant Contact that can personalize each delivery with a "Dear Joe" salutation. I save articles in a digital folder and decide which are most appropriate to include or reference in a monthly e-newsletter.

To take this suggestion one step further, consider producing your own e-newsletter. There are many simple, low-cost e-newsletter software programs available nowadays in addition to the one referenced above. Why wait for an editor to publish you when you can do it yourself? If you do not have a talent for writing, outsource the newsletter to a professional writer (ideally a fellow certified business) who will collaborate with you on content. You can use an e-newsletter to provide updates on your company's activities, provide tips for your customers, and promote events at which you or your staff will be speaking. Don't forget to link your article to your Facebook account and LinkedIn groups.

When creating and writing an e-newsletter, experts advise the following:

- Be very careful to send the e-newsletter only to people who have "opted in" and agreed to receive it. Federal regulations are becoming very strict against spam e-mails. You must also have an opt-out option.
- Be consistent with your delivery frequency. E-newsletters that appear at regular intervals, such as biweekly or monthly, are most likely to become must-reads for the recipients. However, avoid sending e-newsletters too frequently, so your readers don't feel bombarded.
- HTML is recommended, but stay away from too many bells and whistles. These frustrate recipients with slower modem speeds and can also distract from the text you are presenting.
- Everyone loves quick and easy statistics and tips that relate to the product or service universe, so these are a good first line in your newsletter. People will open the letter just to get the quote, tip, or fact of the month.
- Interview clients, association members, fellow MWBEs, and others for inclusion in your e-newsletter. This will provide additional expert contact and show your strong relationships in the business world. As a bonus, if you feature them in your e-news, they are likely to return the favor and feature you.
- Include your contact information prominently on the e-mail, so readers can get in touch with you easily.

Catching the Big Fish: Marketing

- Copyright your newsletter, and display the © symbol. This will protect your original work.

Volunteer.

Giving back is not only good for the soul, it is good for business. Each year, a prominent WBE is the volunteer organizer for a silent auction that benefits the Women's Business Enterprise National Council. Their important efforts benefit us at WBENC and provide the WBE with the opportunity to call corporations to ask for donations, introducing and subtly promoting herself, her company, and her leadership relationship with WBENC. I got my biggest client of the year last year by volunteering for my university's Capital Campaign Committee.

Give media interviews.

If you are lucky, all of the above actions can lead to media interviews that provide additional visibility for your company. WBE and board member Lynthia Romney of RomneyCom, LLC, has placed clients in major broadcast and print media, including the *New York Times*, the *Wall Street Journal*, CNN, *Good Morning America*, and *Bloomberg BusinessWeek*. She has trained hundreds of CEOs, executives, and rising stars on how to build powerful key messages and prepare for interviews. Lynthia recommends the following:

CHEAT SHEET

TIPS FOR PREPARING FOR A MEDIA INTERVIEW

Know what you are going to say and stick with it.

- Effective spokespeople are fluent in the three to five key points they want to make—before they walk into an interview. They know that preparation is 90 percent of success.

- Take the time to plot out a strategic and logical presentation of your ideas and point of view. These should reflect your expertise and distinctive strengths. At the same time, speak to the audience in crisp, memorable language.

Take leadership in the conversation.

- Just because the reporter is asking the question doesn't mean you can't manage the conversation. Stay focused on the points you want to make, and tie them consistently to the themes of her questions.

- Professional and clear advance communications with the reporter or producer will lay the groundwork for a smooth and engaging interview.

Rehearse and rehearse again.

- Confidence is crucial to on-camera credibility. Practice in advance so you are comfortable with your messages.

Be camera-conscious.

- Your visual presence is magnified on screen. Convey your self-assurance with a fixed posture; keep your eyes on the interviewer or camera lens; and smile between questions. A subtle nod signals you are engaged and ready to answer.

Catching the Big Fish: Marketing

> **Tie your comments to a newsworthy event or trend.**
>
> - Broadcast news has a 24/7 appetite. Contextualize your expertise in terms of what is happening in the world. Help the reporter out by offering commentary or data on a trend or news event. And enjoy your role as a subject matter expert.

SEVENTH COMMANDMENT: BE HIGH TOUCH AS WELL AS HIGH TECH

Market yourself in person.

Marketing at events is one of the most effective tools available to MWBEs. Numerous trade shows and business fairs across the country exist for the sole purpose of marketing certified businesses to supplier diversity professionals. The drawback to event marketing, of course, is the time and expense it takes for you and/or your staff to attend various events and represent your business. The rewards, however, can be instant, as some corporate representatives may visit your booth and invite you in for an appointment on the spot.

Do not regard event participation as time away from your business; rather, see it as moving your business to the conference location. In addition to meeting targeted or new contacts, you will learn up-to-date information from the show's producers and have an opportunity to investigate your competitors and potential alliance partners.

Nancy Allen, president and CEO of the Women's Business Development Council of Florida, believes strongly in the importance of sponsorship at the national level as a marketing tool. "Whenever we do an e-blast out for the two national events, [Summit and Salute and National Conference and Business Fair], we promote the idea of sponsorship. As the Summit and Salute has grown, the cost of sponsorship has not risen, so you get a big bang for your buck." Nancy also believes the summit's size and intimate networking opportunities provide WBE sponsors with an advantage. "It is not as big as the national conference, and you get invited to VIP events where high-level corporate execs are present. It is not a secret, so you have to reply early."

Nancy is also a big supporter of the host committee sponsorship opportunity for WBENC's annual NCBF. "I always say to the host committee, 'Look what you get for your sponsorship.'" Former host committee sponsors Terri Hall and Lynn Griffith agree and are more than pleased with the publicity and relationships they built as host committee members. Nancy says, "Both women spoke at an outreach meeting and talked about their experience, and at the meeting's end, we had four people sign up."

Terri was recently featured as a success story on the cover of WBENC's monthly "President's Report" as well. She reports that her $7,500 sponsorship translated to $100,000 in new business. For fellow host committee members, she has designed trade fair booths; for one she is working long term on a rebranding campaign. As is frequently true with these sponsorship investments, Terri has built long-term relationships.

For much more on event marketing advice, see the next chapter, on networking.

EIGHTH COMMANDMENT: SOLICIT AND USE THY ENDORSEMENTS

Satisfied customers provide some of the best and most effective marketing messages available. Get in the habit of collecting endorsements—in the form of short testimonial blurbs or full-length letters—from happy customers, suppliers, employees, partners, and industry experts. Solicit endorsements on LinkedIn and then promote them on Facebook and in your e-newsletter. Most people will be more than willing to support you. "May I have that in writing?" should be your response to compliments. Be sure to save all testimonials and thank-you notes, whether hard copy or electronic, in an easily retrievable file labeled "Endorsements."

As you collect endorsements, use them strategically in your marketing materials. For example, you might include a full range of testimonials on your website to show the diversity of your client base, but include only corporate testimonials in a brochure or media kit targeting a Fortune 500 purchaser. These are especially good to have on hand when you are creating or updating your marketing materials. Also consider a rotating banner on your website with an endorsement of the month.

NINTH COMMANDMENT: DO NOT BE AFRAID TO GO BACK TO THY WELL

One of the best lessons I have learned from reading business guru Tom Peters's books is the effective marketing strategy of seeking and winning more and more business from the same company. As you build and refine your marketing messages, do not be afraid to return and "re-market" to companies who may have rejected your business in the past or to expand your offering to a single customer. Remember that corporations are enormous entities with many nooks and crannies needing new products and services all the time.

Your new certification or its renewal is the perfect moment to revisit a potential customer relationship from your past. Or, if you were already doing business with a particular company before you received your certification, your new status may help you expand that business. Perhaps you have added a new NAICS code; brag about it. All your fishing need not take place in uncharted waters.

TENTH COMMANDMENT: ALWAYS MAKE TIME TO MARKET

I can hear the voices in your head: "I know marketing is very important, but how can I find the time to do all of this time-consuming marketing when I barely have time to blink?" I tell people that I have been marketing all of my professional life, ever since my first post-college position, when I sold the love of reading to eighth-graders as a teacher. Nonetheless, when I changed fields two years ago after a long career in the nonprofit world to be a real-estate agent in New York City, I hired a coach. Under his tutelage and prodding, I follow a rigorous program of personal notes, phone calls, e-mails, mailings, and "pop-bys." Invest in yourself; it is the most important thing you do for your business.

Here are some additional tips from overworked entrepreneurs on how to make time for marketing:

- Attempt to engage in at least one marketing activity every single day. Marketing should appear on every to-do list you have.
- Get your staff to help. If you do not have an employee (or several) dedicated to marketing you and your business, assign this responsibility to someone on your team. If you would prefer, hire a marketing consultant (there are many in the WBENC database) to advise you. In either case, schedule regular meetings with your key staff where only marketing issues will be discussed.
- Take your marketing advice in doses. Sign up for free e-newsletters on the subject of marketing, and set aside thirty minutes per week to review the advice, tips, and strategies in these publications. Or sign up for one marketing seminar every quarter. With the growth in online learning, you may not even need to leave your desk for the class.
- Hire a coach.
- Engage a buddy, and prod one another to market daily.

11TH COMMANDMENT: REMEMBER THAT NETWORKING IS MARKETING

Finally, remember that even the most exquisite marketing brochure in the world is no match for having a personal

Catching the Big Fish: Marketing

connection with a potential customer. Networking may be the most important piece of your marketing pie. It is so important, in fact, that it merits an entire chapter all its own. Read on.

Using social media as part of your strategy.

Susie Aubuchon of McKinley Marketing provides the following advice:

Have a consistent policy throughout your online and social media presence to educate, engage, and activate.

> **Educate**—This is basic brand awareness. You are educating about your brand, what it is, and why it is the best. Make certain you are in a relevant place (in a LinkedIn group, for example, or on Facebook) and saying the right things. You will build your community by "likes" on Facebook or people asking to link to you on LinkedIn. In today's world, if you are not in "social," you don't exist. The top one hundred brands are on all social media because they know it is crucial for reaching their consumer.
>
> **Engage**—This is the heart of social media; you have a direct line to your customers. Its value is second only to your sales force. You need to understand how important this piece is to your marketing campaign. Consumers reach out to companies just as companies reach out to them. It is interactive; you are not just pushing out.
>
>> Engagement takes thought and planning to be effective. The content has to be what someone wants to read. Focus on relevant topics. For example, Colgate might talk about gum disease: "We saw this study that might be of interest; does anyone know other things that work well?" Content does not have to be a sales pitch.
>>
>> The payoff is that you are building your community. How you engage depends on what type of company you are.

Include ways to connect in all your media: your website, your Facebook page, your e-mail signature that says, "friend me on Facebook" or "Get your free weekly white paper" or "Follow us on Twitter and get a weekly coupon." These things give the members of your community reasons to come back to your website or wall.

Activate—This is the call to action. Use social media as a platform for promotions, such as "Use your coupon today and we will contribute 20 percent of the proceeds to..." or "Come to our opening of our new location." Depending on your service, promote online or offline events here. This goes far beyond an online store. Your goal is to develop brand activists. They will effectively help your efforts. They will share your story with their friends, and that brings more people to your site.

Donna Wertalik, faculty and career adviser in marketing at Pamplin College of Business, Virginia Tech, cautions that when you use social networking for business, remember that "the body [company] is the brand; social media is just the vehicle. The fans are followers—it is not a network; it is not going to move your business. As a customer, I need to understand the message from influencers. Instead of going out to a hundred, go out to ten core people who are trusted in their community and go out to their networks. The goal is to change behavior, awareness, and belief."

CASE STUDY

Patty Klein, President and CEO, A-Plus Meetings & Incentives

The value proposition for A-Plus Meetings & Incentives is clear: superior service. They are not your typical event-management company by any standard. The firm serves Fortune 500 companies, including Staples, DHL, Ryder, Armstrong, Scholastic,

Biomet 3i, and Allstate. The company's leaders include former McKinsey and Bain consultants with MBA degrees from Harvard and Wharton. CEO Patty Klein understands that the quality of the meeting planners is exceptionally important to the satisfaction of the attendees.

The company provides true full-service meeting planning, including airline ticketing, registration, graphic arts, and production services. Here is their promise to provide:

Exceptional service for both for planners and attendees. They even guarantee their service.

Personal agendas: These are not just generic agendas with attendee names at the top. Real personal agendas tell each person exactly where he or she needs to be at any moment, including rehearsals, special breakfasts, photo sessions, and so on.

Incentives include fixed, per couple, incentive pricing; dining reservations at all restaurants prior to arrival at the resort; creation of all-inclusive plans at EP resorts.

Full general contractor: They provide one point of contact for travel, production, audiovisual, décor, food and beverage, offsite events, and more, including cutting-edge technologies such as mobile applications.

Cost savings: They offer lower fees, but more importantly, lower costs on every line item for the program.

They're fast, and you'll know it. Not only will you have complete time lines and deadlines, you'll also see how quickly they can turn things around with tight time frames.

Complete budgetary transparency: You'll have full, line-item budgets with detailed backup.

A-Plus applied for and received its certification in 2008. The company had a long history and evolved from its original roots as a travel school that trained travel agents. Later they added a travel agency, a great background for the value they provide in both their meeting planning and their incentive business.

Patty served on a customer advisory board for Staples for fifteen years, so she was well aware of their culture and their needs, and they have been a client since 1997. As with many entrepreneurs, Patty says that it happened by accident, through a friend. The friend was starting an advisory board for Staples and did not know how to do it, so Patty stepped in to help.

That first company was sold in 2000, and Patty stayed with the firm and moved to Florida. During this time, she sat in on a lot of customer advisory boards with the CPOs of Bank of America, Home Depot, Wells Fargo, Pfizer, and Verizon, to name a few. There she learned firsthand of the corporations' desire to purchase from diverse companies.

In the beginning, Patty says, "We planned meetings and served as the facilitator for customer-only groups." Their background in top business schools and their reputation as the cream of the consulting world made them unusual in the meeting planning space, giving them a unique ability to facilitate, plan, and negotiate.

In 2008, Patty and her team left that company, started A-Plus, and immediately contacted WBENC to become certified. Patty says, "All of the clients came with us. We provided free service to these companies through the execution of their events that already had contracts with our prior company to make certain everything went well." This type of service is the hallmark of the company and is reflected in the referrals, endorsements, and praise they receive from all their clients.

According to Patty, "Certification has opened doors and helped us get into the RFP process. In 2009, WBENC went out to bid on the Summit and Salute. Forty-five WBEs bid. We won the business and have kept it. We believe we were selected because we could bring a strategic and marketing perspective. We also bring exceptional service to the event. We approach this in the same manner as a corporate high-touch event."

This is certainly endorsed by the top client, Staples, which says this of A-Plus:

- Your unique ability to get to know your client and understand the business they are in.

- Going over and above with client requests—no is never an answer with you.

- Your willingness to do things other meeting planners would never do. such as

    o Seeing off or greeting clients, *regardless of what time it is*

    o Personally carrying baggage and bringing clients up to their rooms (this always amazes our guests)

    o Getting clients whatever they need, even if it means going offsite for something

- The ease of working with you; you do your job so well that you make it easier for the corporate planner"

Patty continues, "The WBENC business was a great chance to demonstrate our service and strategic approach to corporations who attend these programs. Our service is personal; we greet people, carry the bags, show the room, and so on. We hope our WBENC attendees can go back to their internal meeting sponsors and incentive leaders and say 'We saw them in action, and they are great. You should include them in the next RFP.'"

Patty hopes that this strategy will lead to more business for the company and states: "Meeting planning is a great area for diversity spend. We are a woman-owned firm, but we are also the thirtieth largest meeting planning company in the country with $14 million in tier-one spend." Patty believes it is a no-risk decision for the corporations, as it is CEOs and division heads that are their references.

Chapter Four

Networking

To say that I am an enthusiastic proponent of networking is a bit of an understatement. My husband, Dick, jokes that whenever I enter a room, I start a receiving line. One of the things I love about my real-estate business is that everywhere I go and everything I do is networking for my business. Networking must be part of your skill set if you want to build a successful company.

Think you are too busy running your business to make time for networking? Think again. As the CEO of your company, getting your face "out there" is an important part of your position description.

Even if you feel content with the current direction of your business, networking exposes you to a whole new world of possibilities. Consistent networking led me to one of the most exciting opportunities of my career. In the early 1980s, I held a presidential appointment in the Reagan Administration as the director of the Institute of Museum Services. My main contact in the White House Office of Presidential Personnel was a woman named Maryann Urban. At one of the dozens of receptions I took the time to attend each month, I saw Maryann and went up to chat with her.

"What's new?" I asked.

Maryann responded to my simple question by confiding that she was moving to Pennsylvania in two weeks to be closer to her significant other.

"But Maryann," I said, "if you leave the White House, who will be my contact?"

"Would you like my job?" she replied.

The next day I received a call from her boss, Bob Tuttle, and a week later I was sitting at my new desk in the old Executive Office Building with the title of associate director of presidential personnel. As a result of that move, I later added the title of chairman of the President's Committee on Women Business Enterprise, the first step on my path to WBENC. This huge career opportunity arose because I had built strong, trusting relationships and I had shown up. That's networking.

As an interesting side note, I ran into Maryann in Pennsylvania when I represented WBENC at a joint Department of Labor/White House conference for women business owners. This time Maryann approached me and shared the fact that she had married her significant other and that she was running her own business.

I could share dozens of other networking stories, as could many of my colleagues and friends. Much has been written and discussed about networking, yet I am often surprised at how few business owners possess a true grasp of how to network effectively. Networking must be fully integrated into the daily operations of your business, not considered an extracurricular activity. Trust me, the more you do it, the easier and more rewarding it becomes. As this chapter will demonstrate, many successful WBEs landed their biggest corporate customers through—you guessed it—networking.

First, let me address some of the common misconceptions held by skeptical business owners:

- Networking is *not* attending unlimited luncheons to collect and distribute as many business cards as humanly possible.
- Networking is *not* joining sixty-five associations and never attending any events.
- Networking is *not* meeting people and telling them what *they* can do for *you*.
- Networking is *not* posting a comment on Facebook.
- Networking is *not* something to be dreaded.

Networking

Networking is, quite simply, the building and nurturing of professional relationships, live and in person. While social networks are a good addition to your marketing plan when well thought out and executed, they cannot replace the person-to-person interaction of networking. Your network of contacts is one of your most valuable assets as a business owner. And remember, networking is not just about who you know, it is about who knows *you*. If you are new to the world of supplier diversity, you absolutely must network to make yourself known. Your certification is just the first step in the process and is meaningless if you do not put it to work.

Woody Allen once said, "Eighty percent of success is showing up." I can attest to the validity of that statement. When I was president of WBENC, I traveled quite a bit and tried to attend the business fairs and conferences of WBENC's affiliate organizations and the many other business-focused groups with which we maintained cooperative relationships. Just as you market your company, I walked the floor of the shows, introducing myself and WBENC or just saying hello to WBENC members and prospect companies.

At one such event, I stopped by the Kellogg booth to say hello to Cathy Kutch, the head of their supplier diversity program. I had talked with her on many occasions and had pitched her on Kellogg's joining WBENC as a corporate member. Unexpectedly, she turned to me and said, "I see you at all of these supplier diversity events and appreciate the fact that you support other organizations." She then told me to send her an invoice for corporate membership. Cathy and Kellogg remain an active member of the organization today.

This worked for WBE Rosalie Edson and her happy customer Pitney Bowes. Rosalie, the CEO of Meadows Office Furniture, is as good a networker as I have met. Always charming and funny, she also gives back and is remembered by all who meet her. In addition to sponsoring WPEO and WBENC events, Rosalie hosts an annual WPEO event at the Haworth showroom.

Laura Taylor, WBENC board chair and Pitney Bowes vice president, attended those events. Laura says that Rosalie was in the right place at the right time. "We were doing a renovation of our headquarters. Through WBENC, we were able to connect Meadows to our corporate real-estate VP. Pitney Bowes was looking to change its working environment, and Meadows, with their design knowledge about trends in the way people work in a business environment and association with Haworth, was able to come in and provide a total solution."

Rosalie says, "We understand the mindset of corporate America, and the challenges that they have in these economic times. It was great to work with the Pitney Bowes team. Belonging to WBENC has opened up a whole new understanding of teamwork."

This chapter offers the most effective networking activities for building your reputation and relationships in the world of supplier diversity. While many of the networking techniques in this chapter apply to any business owner, keep in mind that WBEs face special networking challenges and enjoy unique opportunities.

The biggest challenge to networking in this community is its size. While corporate America is big, the corporate supplier diversity community is not. Supplier diversity professionals are a tight-knit group, and their numbers are relatively small, consisting of about a thousand people across the country. This means that first impressions are important and less-than-stellar first impressions can be difficult to overcome.

I must say that just about everyone I have met in the diversity community is both very kind and passionately dedicated to helping MWBEs succeed (and you can see this in the valuable advice they share in this book). Supplier diversity professionals are your advocates; as you read in chapter two, it is their job to help you. However, the truth is that they are more likely to help you if you have built a relationship with them. We are all overworked, and our time is always double booked, so the phone calls we return are the calls from people we have met, know about, and want to talk to.

How do you make yourself known and appreciated? Show up! You *must* attend business fairs, trade shows, association meetings, and other events to meet and build relationships with supplier diversity professionals, WMBE organizations, and your sister certified businesses. The good news is that the supplier diversity community offers abundant opportunities for business owner Davids to meet corporate Goliaths. Meet and greet opportunities are part of the industry's standard practice.

Throughout this chapter, keep in mind that just like your marketing activities, your networking tactics must be strategic and consistent to be effective. Association dues, trade show fees, and high-tech database management systems can be expensive and time consuming, so educate yourself about all the available opportunities, and then pick and choose what will work for your particular business and industry segment.

All MWBEs—and all M/WBE networking practices—need not be the same. Patty Klein, CEO of A-Plus Meetings & Incentives, says, "You don't need appointments to make connections. It's all about meeting the folks and networking. Don't be afraid to walk up to someone and introduce yourself. You never know where it will lead."

Sometimes networking is paired successfully with learning opportunities. According to Ohio WBE Pam Ward, president of Graphics Continuum, Inc., "'Thursday Religion' is the best way for me to describe the diversity meeting held each week at UC Health. The business sermons, as I call them, consist of open discussions on current business topics that have been invaluable as I grow my business. As a busy, certified women-owned, small-business owner, it is sometimes difficult for me to find the time each week to attend these two hour meetings, but I have come to realize these weekly business meetings are a workshop with top executives at no cost. I try to make it a priority. I consider this time my time to listen, think, learn best practices, and hear how others are handling their growth and financial needs. Over the last two years, not only have I made good friends, but my business portfolio has grown. I have successfully done work for UC Health and fourteen other corporate attendees."

Finally, remember to relax and have a bit of fun while you are networking. Making genuine connections with other businesspeople in the supplier diversity community can be one of the most rewarding and enjoyable aspects of business ownership. Most of these professionals are passionate about their work and derive enormous satisfaction from helping to maximize each other's success.

GETTING TO KNOW YOU: ASSOCIATIONS AND NETWORKING ORGANIZATIONS

As a place to get started, WBENC has formal agreements with the following organizations that share an interest in enhancing business opportunities and professional development for women business owners and entrepreneurs.

NATIONAL MOU AND AFFINITY PARTNERS

WBENC's affinity partners include other business advocacy organizations for minorities and women, industry-specific organizations, government agencies, and trade associations. You can find their websites by visiting www.wbenc.org.

- Airport Minority Advisory Council (AMAC)
- Business and Professional Women (BPW)
- Center for Women's Business Research (CWBR)
- Count Me In (CMI)
- Institute for Supply Management (ISM)
- Latina Style Magazine

Networking

- National Association of Asian American Business Associations (NAABA)
- National Association of Minority and Women-Owned Law Firms (NAMWLF)
- National Association of Regulatory Utility Commissioners (NARUC)
- National Association of Women Business Owners (NAWBO)
- National Association of Women in Construction (NAWIC)
- National Association of Veteran-Owned Businesses (NAVOWB)
- National Gay and Lesbian Chamber of Commerce (NGLCC)
- National Minority Supplier Development Council (NMSDC)
- National Women's Business Council (NWBC)
- US Hispanic Chamber of Commerce (USHCC)
- US Business Leadership Network (USBLN)
- US Pan Asian American Chamber of Commerce (USPAAC)
- Women Construction Owners and Executives (WCOOE)
- Women Impacting Public Policy (WIPP)
- Women Presidents' Organization (WPO)

WBENC GLOBAL PARTNERSHIPS

WEConnect International

WEConnect International works with a global network to help facilitate sustainable economic growth by increasing opportunities for women-owned businesses to succeed in the global value chain.

The WEConnect International network represents over $700 billion in annual purchasing power. Founding members include Accenture, Alcatel-Lucent, AT&T, Boeing, Cisco Systems, Citigroup, Ernst & Young, HP, IBM, Intel, Manpower, Motorola,

Pfizer, PG&E, Verizon, and Walmart. These corporations are world leaders in promoting more inclusive global value chains.

WEConnect International recognizes that WBENC Standards and Procedures are the gold standard for women's business enterprise (WBE) certification. Like WBENC, WEConnect international certifies WBEs that are at least 51 percent owned, managed, and controlled by one or more women. The two organizations are collaborating to make it easier for women business owners to find each other, do business together, and scale their businesses globally.

Technology plays a pivotal role in this new network to help compress the procurement cycle and transcend some of the traditional barriers to trade.

WEConnect International works closely with several supporting organizations to help deliver on its mission and services, including WEConnect Canada, WEConnect Europe, NASSCOM in India, Quantum Leaps, the Women Presidents' Organization, the World Bank Group, the International Trade Centre, and other champions in key markets.

WECONNECT INTERNATIONAL AND WBENC

The certification process followed by WEConnect International is modeled on WBENC's Standards and Procedures. The Women's Business Enterprise National Council certifies WBEs in the United States, and WEConnect International certifies WBEs based outside of the United States

The WEConnect relationship has greatly increased the international programming of the RPOS, with several having Global Good Morning events that either stand alone or are incorporated into annual conferences.

According to Blanca Robinson, executive director of the Women's Business Enterprise Council South, based in New Orleans,

In 2010 the executive director from the Newfoundland and Labrador Organization for Women Entrepreneurs (NLOWE), an affiliate of WEConnect Canada, contacted me mid-fourth quarter. She wanted to begin a dialogue on how Canadian businesses could do business with US businesses and wanted to come down on a reconnaissance mission. This was right before our annual holiday luncheon, so I invited her to come and join us and provided time on the program for her to speak about their organization.

Within two months, we set up a trade mission. Several of their businesses came to New Orleans, and we set up MatchMaker meets with both corporations and WBE firms in the oil and gas industry. It was very successful, and they came back to our 2012 expo. They wanted to be a sponsor, so we created Global Good Morning. The program included a presentation from the Department of Commerce for women who want to do business internationally and from the Canadian consulate about business opportunities with Canada.

We had hoped to have forty-five or fifty people attend, and actually had over two hundred who registered. There was a good mix of corporate and WBEs and women from NLOWE."

Other RPOs have experienced similar success. Astra's President Diane McClelland is expanding their global programming after the positive response to their first programs. "Astra's Global Initiative started in 2008 and has been building momentum and focus. It had its first face-to-face Trade Mission in February 2012 with WEConnect-Canada. In addition to the consul general of Canada and representatives of the office of the Secretary of State, there were seventeen trade delegates from Canada and more than twenty-five from the United States.

For our next program, the Women Entrepreneurs Global Connect Expo and Summit, we are again asking WEConnect

International to attend and are inviting women business owners from Korea, China, India, Malaysia, Vietnam, and Canada to come and meet with Astra and other WBENC WBEs to explore doing business together and or/partnering for larger contracts with Fortune 500 companies.

One of the first steps to building a good network is to join organizations that offer opportunities to meet and connect with other businesspeople with which you share an industry, community, or other affinity. Hundreds of thousands of organizations exist—some as small as five or six people, others as large as many corporations. Depending on your interests, business needs, and time availability, many associations and networking groups are likely to appeal to you.

WHERE TO START?

Given all these options, how do you decide which memberships are worthwhile? There is no correct number of association memberships to have, so you will have to decide what makes sense for you. Some business owners belong to only one or two associations and become extremely active, while others find value in receiving the publications and membership benefits of several additional organizations.

Here are some suggestions for vetting which associations and networking groups are worth the membership dues. Keep these tips in mind as you read through the organizations described on the next several pages.

- **Ask friends and colleagues** in your industry what associations they belong to and/or recommend. If it seems as though "everyone" belongs, then you should too.
- **Seek the guidance** of corporate supplier diversity professionals, as you begin to develop relationships with them. Many corporations recognize the competitive advantage association membership can provide to their

Networking

suppliers, and they will recommend certain memberships over others.
- **Visit the website** of each association (and each association's local chapter if applicable) you are considering. Check closely for information about the following:
    - *Membership dues*—Be on the lookout for lower prices if you join for multiple years at one time, or if your join during a special membership drive.
    - *Membership benefits*—Often the benefits available to association members, such as a free subscription to industry publications or discounts on event attendance, justify the annual membership dues.
    - *Publications*—Does the association offer members a magazine, app, or e-newsletter? As discussed in the previous chapter on marketing, industry publications are one of the best ways to educate yourself about your potential customers and competitors and to promote yourself as a contributor or interview subject. Pay special attention to the corporations that advertise in these publications.
    - *Events and workshops*—How often does the association host conferences and networking events or educational workshops in your area? Does the organization host webinars? Will membership guarantee you will receive invitations to these events? Are there separate fees to attend these events, and can nonmembers attend at a higher price?
    - *Membership directory or database*—If you join this association, will you receive either a hardcopy directory of members or passcode access to a database? The latter is obviously more likely to be kept up to date. Will you be able to promote yourself to your fellow members or are their restrictions on such activities?

- *Special interest groups*—If the association is particularly large, does it offer smaller affinity groups that meet your particular needs? For instance, do they offer a women's group, a marketers' group, a finance group, an international group, and so on. Often these special-interest groups have their own area on the association's website, their own meetings, and their own publications. For example, the National Association of Women in Construction has separate activities and opportunities for entrepreneurial members.
- *Board of directors*—Who sits on the association's board? These VIPs can offer insight into the caliber and influence of the organization.
- *Take a test drive*—While most associations do not offer trial memberships, it is worthwhile to call and request free attendance at an event or a free copy of the association's most recent communication so you can check them out before committing to any high-cost membership dues.

Keeping the above issues in mind, here is a comprehensive guide to the wide variety of organizations that exist and the opportunities each offers to MWBEs interested in selling to large corporations.

Industry Associations

If you haven't already, I highly recommend that you join the most prominent trade association in your industry. From the National Electrical Manufacturer's Association to the Women's Food Forum to the International Franchise Association to the Independent Computer Consultants Association to the American Translators Association, I can virtually guarantee that a trade group exists, no matter what your field. (For a comprehensive list of over 6,500 associations, visit the "Gateway to Associations" on the website of the American Society of Association Executives at www.asaenet.org.)

Some industry associations offer the option to join a local chapter, while others provide their services from a single national headquarters. Larger industries often have a few competing associations serving their community. It is perfectly fine (though not always necessary) to join all associations in your industry, depending on your needs, budget, and time constraints.

The main advantages of industry association membership include highly specialized publications and educational opportunities, mentoring programs to learn from more-experienced professionals in your field (or to give back to those just starting out), and political lobbying on behalf of your group's interests.

Most industry associations collect data on pricing policies, industry-specific government regulations, salaries, and trends that can be enormously helpful. Your membership dues may be repaid many times over by access to this information.

Organizations for Certified Businesses

Joining an organization in this category should not require any thought—it is 100 percent essential to take advantage of this networking gold mine. As advised earlier, upon receiving your certification, you should make contact with the regional or local affiliate (RPO—regional partner organization for WBENC-certified businesses) that processed your certification. Simply call and introduce yourself and ask for a calendar of upcoming events in your area. Most likely, you will have been added to the e-blast list the organization uses to inform certified businesses about upcoming programs and opportunities that they host or that are hosted by the corporate sponsors in a locale. Even if you are already receiving these communications, it pays to make personal contact by phone or in person at an event with one of the staff members. Connection to these groups will ensure that you have access to expert advice and the most current resources available regarding supplier diversity in your region.

Note: If you do not personally review the e-mails that come into your company, make certain that the person designated to receive your e-mails notifies you of these important business opportunities. At a minimum, in addition to notices of trade shows, workshops, and webinars hosted by your RPO, read the WBENC "President's Report" to keep on top of programs and opportunities.

WBENC and its regional affiliates provide a variety of networking opportunities to businesses holding certifications. As you will recall from previous chapters, WBENC's affiliates include Regional Partner Organizations (RPO's). These RPOs, some of which charge separate membership dues or event fees (above and beyond the certification fee that they collect to process your certification and conduct a site visit) provide highly specialized advice and networking opportunities for certified women business enterprises. Note that the RPOs that charge a membership fee return that part of the fee (but not the nonrefundable processing fee) if you are denied certification.

Each of these RPOs (as listed in appendix A), has a Women's Enterprise Leadership Forum made up of WBEs who share the desire to expand their contracting opportunities with America's corporations. If you are a WBENC-certified WBE, I highly recommend that you join a local forum. You can apply for national forum membership through your RPO or submit a request to WBENC President Pamela Eason. National forum meetings and local forum events are high-level networking opportunities where connections are made that lead to business opportunities.

Nine national forum members serve on the WBENC Board of Directors for three-year terms. Every WBENC-certified business is eligible for this exclusive access, so do not be shy about raising your hand for a forum opportunity.

According to Dell's Kim Brown, WBEs should "actively engage in WBENC at the national and regional partner level. Take advantage of the opportunities to serve these organizations along the side of supplier diversity professionals. As you serve, you will develop strong relationships. The supplier diversity professionals are your champions inside the targeted corporation. They will work with you to identify the right opportunity for introduction and make introductions for you. In some instances, you may find an immediate opportunity in the company. In most instances, it takes much longer to identify the right opportunity for your company. The timing of the introduction is critical, as there are many variables.

Dell also has its own programs dedicated to women business owners.

One such program is Empowering Women in Technology and Business. According to the Dell blog, Direct2Dell:

> While women share a unique perspective and approach to business, technology enables businesses everywhere to use data and reach customers in unprecedented ways. What's important is not the technology itself, but what it enables you to do.
>
> Dell's Women Powering Business initiative strives to help women entrepreneurs and technologists expand their networks while offering capabilities to help them use technology to do more. You can join other female business leaders from around the globe via Twitter and LinkedIn as w celebrate the impact of women-owned businesses on the global economy.

As you can see, the most obvious benefit of certification-related organizations is the targeted nature of their mission. Leaders of these groups know that their business-owner members want to network with corporate purchasing executives, so they regularly provide such opportunities. For instance, my own RPO, the Women Presidents' Educational Organization of the New York region, run by Marsha Firestone, PhD, sponsors an annual Breakthrough Breakfast at which certified WBEs interact with a few dozen corporate purchasing officers. Their more than thirteen thousand Done Deals are celebrated both between corporations and WBEs and WBE-WBE deals. (Done Deals are executed contracts between a corporation or government agency and a WBE or a WBE-WBE deal.)

Throughout the year, all of the RPOs conduct corporate/WBE networking events that range from educational panels and seminars to multiday business fairs and conferences. The president of the Women's Business Council Southwest, Debbie Hurst, reminds us that they provide four major events each year. They host the largest procurement event in the Southwest (businessWorks) and the biggest recognition event (the Parade of Stars Gala). They also hold Harvesting Partnerships, an education symposium, which includes the Lillie Knox Memorial Luncheon, where they present cash awards of up to $5,000 for the Lillie Knox Investing for Growth Award. The WBC-Southwest is actually the originator of the Done Deals program, and they report out their Done Deals at Power to Potential held in the late fall. After the general session, workshops are held that address the engagement process, opportunities, and how to do business with corporations, government, and WBE to WBE.

WBENC's e-newsletter "President's Report," contains up-to-date information on events across the country all year. Check the RPOs' websites regularly to stay current on new opportunities (Go to http://www.wbenc.org/schedule/calendarfull.asp?id=250&category=All for a full listing.) Many successful WBEs attend the events of many of the RPOs, not just their local group.

WBENC's own National Conference and Business Fair is held annually at the end of June. The four-day event, chock-full of formal and informal networking opportunities, is a business networker's paradise. The first day features the annual meeting of The Forum. Networking opportunities include the chance to get to know women CEOs whose own purchasing programs often rival those of the corporations and who often provide second-tier opportunities as well.

The conference also offers workshops, plenary sessions, and receptions that impart valuable information while providing the opportunity to meet corporate representatives. Wednesday of conference week is dedicated to the business fair, where more than four hundred exhibitors set up booths and provide opportunities throughout the day for business interaction. Even the breakfasts, lunches, and evening events provide forums for WBEs and corporate purchasing and supplier diversity executives to meet and exchange information. On Thursday, prescheduled one-on-one MatchMaker Meetings (see chapter five for more information on these opportunities) start things off, and workshops provide cutting-edge information on supply-chain trends and practices.

Success stories abound about WBEs that regularly attend the offerings of their RPO. Geri Swift, president of Women's Business Enterprise Council PA-DE-sNJ adds that "all of our programs have an educational component—they are effective, they have a theme, and a direct result is that everyone walks away with something. One of the things we have done to enrich the experience is to create the Envoy Group. WBEs volunteer to assist other WBEs when they come to the programs. They help the corporations as well. At our executive leadership luncheons, envoys sit at each table and help to facilitate the discussion. Attendees share best practices and learn from each other how to better utilize their certification as a marketing tool."

This process has led to great benefits for WBEs and corporations alike. Geri continues: "An example would be Ellen Lutz, who said that the best thing that ever happened to her was when she came to a program and sat next to First Energy's Tabitha Stanislaw. It turned out that First Energy had a specific need for what her company does, and she got a contract.

"We held an event in Pittsburgh sponsored by the Pittsburgh Pirates on how to do business with Major League Baseball. WBE Carol Philip of CPI Creative sat with the supplier diversity representative and not only became a supplier; she was subsequently honored as diverse supplier of the year."

I remember Carol and her company because of the fabulous booth, set up as a luncheonette that they created for Office Depot at one of the WBENC national conferences. The visibility resulted in an incredible amount of new business for her company.

Chambers of Commerce

Chambers of commerce provide another easy way to become involved in your local community of entrepreneurs. Chambers include a sampling of businesses of all shapes and sizes in your town or city. Membership dues generally range from a few hundred to a few thousand dollars, based on the size of your business. While you may or may not come across corporate purchasers at meetings of your local chamber, you will connect with contacts that can refer you in the right direction, as well as potential suppliers, partners, advisers, and friends.

Additionally, local chambers host business fairs, workshops, conferences, and other events that can be beneficial in and of themselves or can serve as a nice training ground for the bigger corporate events or trade shows you will attend later. In any big cities, large corporations are active members of the local chamber of commerce.

For more information about chamber membership, specific events, and resources, visit www.uschamber.com.

Large ethnic chambers, such as the US Hispanic Chamber of Commerce (www. ushcc.com) and the National Black Chamber of Commerce (www.nationalbcc.org) provide similar opportunities both regionally and nationally. Susan Au Allen, president and CEO of the US Pan Asian American Chamber of Commerce

Networking

(www.uspaacc.com), invites Asian American business owners to learn more about this organization, saying, "Formed in 1984, the US Pan Asian American Chamber of Commerce is a vital voice for the Pan Asian American business community. We advocate for equal procurement opportunities for Asian Americans before major corporations, government agencies and the US Congress. By opening the doors of contract, professional and educational opportunities to those who seek them, we help to nurture, develop, and grow small businesses into medium-size and then large businesses."

Women and Minority Associations

As more and more women and minorities have taken on leadership roles in business, organizations have formed to provide unique networking and educational opportunities within these communities. Some of the larger professional women's groups in this category include the National Association of Women Business Owners (www.nawbo.org), American Business Women's Association (www.abwa.org), Business and Professional Women USA (www.bpwusa.org), and the National Association for Female Executives (www.nafe.com). Large national minority associations, in addition to the chambers listed above, include the Latin Business Association (www.lbausa.com), the National Minority Business Council (www.nmbc.org), and the National Indian Business Association (www.nibanetwork.org).

In addition to these large organizations, which provide networking opportunities among businesses of a wide variety of sizes, industries, and locations, many smaller women's and minority groups exist within industries. Examples include the National Society of Black engineers (www.nsbe.org), the National Association of Minority Contractors (www.namcline.org), Women in Technology International (www.witi.com), and the National Association of Women in Construction (www.nawic.org).

Like industry associations, many women's and minority organizations provide member benefits, conferences and events, publications, leadership opportunities, mentoring programs, and attention to political issues affecting their members. And with any organization, there are great opportunities to make new friends.

Mastermind Groups

Mastermind groups consist of a small number of like-minded business people who meet regularly to share goals and support one another in business success. You can find groups that are industry-specific or include representatives of diverse businesses. Many certified business owners find it helpful to form or join a mastermind group of other certified MWBEs. The sharing of resources, contacts, and advice in an intimate setting can be invaluable.

WBENC Affinity Partner, the Women Presidents' Organization with more than one hundred chapters on four continents, is among the more formal mastermind organizations. I belong to one of several Manhattan chapters. This WPO limits participation in each of its peer mentoring groups to twenty entrepreneurs led by a professional, trained facilitator called a chapter chair. Only businesses that generate at least $2 million in gross annual sales (or $1 million for service-based businesses) are eligible to participate. Additionally, WPO offers Platinum Groups, which bring together WPO members with revenues of $10 million and above and Zenith Groups for businesses with revenues of $50 million or greater to address their specific needs.

If you cannot find an existing mastermind group that suits your needs, go ahead and start your own.

MAKING THE MOST OF YOUR MEMBERSHIPS

Associations exist to serve the needs of members like you, so let them do their job. If you have employees, use your staff strategically—especially your sales team—and assign each to specific associations. Their networking efforts will expand the opportunities for your firm.

Here are several suggestions on how to maximize your organization memberships to help grow your business and attract corporate contacts:

- Say hello. Introduce yourself to the leaders of associations to which you belong on both the national and local levels. Remember, successful networking means that people must know who you are and what you do. Call and say hello, or introduce yourself at an association event. This is one time that you do not want to just send an e-mail. A face-to-face contact is far more memorable. Do not be shy!
- List yourself and your business in member directories. This is another obvious business strategy but often forgotten. As with supplier diversity databases, make sure that your association member listings remain current and fully describe the capabilities of your business. You never know where a potential customer will find you. And be certain to keep electronic databases up-to-date with correct contact information, including changes to your e-mail address.
- Read the member database. Scour the listings of members to find people in the companies or industries you are targeting as customers. I do not recommend cold calling every potential lead in your association, but you may consider a targeted e-mail or direct-mail campaign to key prospects, or ask an association leader to make a personal introduction. If the organization has a LinkedIn group, sign up and follow the posts, adding content when you have something to add to the dialogue. This is also a good place to find suppliers and strategic partners to help you grow your business. (Do not waste money on mailings unless they are professional in appearance and you have a good plan for following up.)

- Join LinkedIn groups. A LinkedIn group from an association is great for discussing current events in your industry and asking for advice and finding support from your peers. And, if you are not in the mood to participate on any given day, all you need to do is click "Delete." They are also a good way to keep in touch with former colleagues who may be helpful in making introductions and generating sales leads. Be careful if you delegate the task of monitoring these discussions to someone on your staff; that person must understand the value to your company of these opportunities and forward information accordingly to the appropriate contact within your company.
- Take an active leadership role. Raise your hand for committees, board positions, and other responsibilities (such as WBENC forums mentioned earlier) that will teach you skills, introduce you to key people in your association, and provide you with opportunities to build your reputation in the organization. Prove yourself to be a visible, responsible leader. Tara Abraham is a good example and has been a Business Star, chair of The Forum, and member of the WBENC board. Everyone in the WBENC network knows Tara, whether they have done business with her or not.
- Contribute to association publications. As discussed, most large associations have multiple online and print publications. Send in your news and press releases for member news areas. Offer to write bylined articles on topics of interest to association members. Call the editor of each publication and volunteer yourself as an "expert" resource on topics related to your business.
- Speak. Connect with the programming director of any organization of which you are a member, and find out the procedure for speaking at an event. Many associations are pleased to present seminars and workshops featuring the expertise of their own members.

Networking

- Apply for awards. Member of the Year, Mentor of the Year, Done Deals, Volunteer of the Year—most associations honor several members annually. Local and national certification organizations offer many impressive award opportunities as well. Winning an award is great publicity that catapults you to visibility and status in your organization, in your community, and in your industry. Even the act of applying demonstrates your motivation to association leaders and award evaluation committees. When you win, do not forget to widely distribute a press release concerning the award or honor, particularly to corporations you are pitching. An added bonus is that accepting the award generally gives you a visible networking opportunity at the award event or ceremony.
- Be charitable. Donate one of your products (or provide a gift certificate if your business does not produce an appropriate item) to an association-sponsored auction. This raises your profile and shows that you are willing to give back to your organization and its members.
- Be a mentor and help other people to meet their goals. I have a cousin who founded his own law firm. At the request of a friend, Robbie, an expert on DNA defenses, spent several meetings with a fifty-four-year old retired and successful entrepreneur who wanted to go back to school to become an attorney so that he too could provide pro bono DNA defenses to unjustly incarcerated individuals. As an afterthought at the conclusion of their second lunch, Robbie asked for advice on how to build a successful business—his law firm. While he was an experienced attorney, "rain making" was new to him. His guest told him to take out a pencil and create a list of ten successful friends—all business owners. He told Robbie to tell these people that he said Robbie was a "first-rate" attorney who should be considered to handle their business's legal needs. Needless to say, the few hours Robbie spent with this gentleman paid off in spades for his new law firm. A friendship was born as well.

Breaking Through

- Buy advertising. If you have the marketing budget and your association includes some of your corporate prospects as members, consider buying classified or full-page advertising in an important industry publication. At a trade show, if you are not going to have a booth or sponsor an event, an advertisement in the trade-show directory will keep you visible.
- Show up again and again. All of the above strategies for maximizing your association memberships will be infinitely more effective the more you show your face at association events and meet your fellow members.

ATTENDING NETWORKING EVENTS

Meetings, conferences, workshops, and social outings are where the very best connections are established and nurtured. Whether attending an event hosted by an association to which you belong or that of another organization, follow these strategies for getting the most out of your attendance:

- Do your homework. Learn as much as you can about the event, sponsoring organization, speakers, and attendees before you attend. Do a Bing or Google search on the name of the keynote speaker; you may learn that he or she sits on the board of your top corporate prospect.
- Send a personal, handwritten note to the CEO of the sponsoring organization, thanking that person for making the event possible and indicating you would like to thank her or him in person at the event.
- Arrive early. The earlier you arrive, the more chances you will have to chat with the organizers of the event and the most eager attendees. You will also have time to get a good seat, read any provided materials, and feel comfortable.
- Mention your membership. Include mention of your certification and/or your association affiliation when you introduce yourself to new people. "My name is Janet Jones,

Networking

and I own a certified Woman Business Enterprise in the garment manufacturing industry."

- Bring materials. In addition to the essential stack of business cards (when in doubt, bring more than you think you will need; there is no excuse for running out of cards and writing on the back of a napkin), go ahead and bring brochures (this is one place where the digital version is not enough), product samples, or other marketing materials. They may stay in your tote bag or briefcase, but you will be happy to have these materials at hand if you meet a strong prospect. Make sure your certification logo appears clearly on all materials. The WBENC seal will be readily recognized and will be an instant signal to any supplier diversity attendees you meet.
- Aside from formal events, I never travel without a stack of business cards in my carry-on luggage. You never know who will be ahead of you in the TSA line or seated next to you on the plane or in the club. Furthermore, if your certification RPO provides pins or other "markers," you should wear them proudly on your lapel as yet another indicator of your status. The new legacy bracelets can form the basis of a long conversation.
- Do not act desperate to make contacts. Recognize that others are evaluating you, so be professional and courteous, and keep a positive attitude at all times.
- Do not go it alone. If you are shy, bring a networking buddy—a fellow businessperson who is not there to keep you company at the buffet, but rather to encourage you to talk to new people. Sometimes a little extra push is all you need.
- Go outside your comfort zone. Even if you are not shy, the danger of being too active in a networking organization is that you will want to spend events chatting with your friends. While it is important to keep up with existing contacts (and by all means spend some time with your pals

and existing customers), make a concerted effort to meet new people at every event you attend.
- Be name-tag savvy. When you can, list both your name and the name of your business on your name tag. Help people connect you and your face with your company. You may even consider purchasing your own name tag to ensure that your name and company name are large enough to be clearly read at a handshake's distance. This also guarantees correct spelling and prevents inappropriate nicknames and other errors.
- Meet the speakers. Go right up and introduce yourself to the event's speakers or panelists. They are there not only to speak but also to network, so do not be shy. Chances are your membership dues and/or sponsorships are helping to pay their speaking fees. If you do feel intimidated, this situation comes with the perfect icebreaker. "I am really looking forward to your talk" works every time. If the speaker has written a book or article, read it in advance so that you can say, "I read your article in *MBE Magazine* and would like to ask…"
- Take notes. Besides writing down interesting information provided in the formal program, take note of the names of people you have met and any follow-up required. You can do this on a tablet or even on the back of their business cards so you remember who is who and what you promised to provide.
- Follow up. Immediately follow up with all important contacts made at a networking function. Preferably within a day or two, but not longer than a week, send a brief e-mail, make a phone call, or send a personal card to keep the relationship going. This is what defines and differentiates smart networkers. I always carry note cards with me and use time on the airplane to write a quick "it was great meeting you." These days, our e-mail in-boxes are usually full, but a personal note is still read. Particularly with

Networking

potential customers, show that you are a person who follows up and keeps your word.
- Keep your promises of "we must get together" with a recommendation of a specific time, place, and activity, and you will end up ahead of the pack. In Manhattan, I belong to a theater club where I frequently get very inexpensive seats to Broadway and off Broadway shows. One of my clients loves theater, and I invite her at least once a quarter to see a show with me.

SUCCESS STORY

JENNIFER COLLINS, PRESIDENT AND CEO OF THE EVENT PLANNING GROUP, LLC

Forum member Jennifer Collins has her own theory on how to break through. She sums it up in one word: *visibility*. "How many people would buy a product or service sight unseen?" Jennifer asks. Since being certified, she

- was introduced by one corporation to another that resulted in a contract ("It took a year, but we remained in front of them.");
- was elected to the WPEO-DC board;
- was a Business Star in 2010;
- chaired the host committee for the 2010 WBENC National Conference and Business Fair;
- participated in the Tuck-WBENC Executive Education Program; and
- serves on The Forum.

In addition, by sponsoring a local Breakthrough Breakfast, Jennifer got her moment on stage where she was able to spotlight herself and her company.

Breaking Through

Jennifer adds, "The point here is that in all of those things, corporations are there. There's an opportunity to have casual conversations where you can really get to know them and they can get to know you. They all give you visibility."

NETWORKING NIRVANA: SUPPLIER DIVERSITY TRADE SHOWS, AND BUYERS MARTS

Early in my career, when I was a manufacturer's representative covering a six-state New England territory, I attended my industry's national annual trade show at the Waldorf-Astoria Hotel in New York City. It was great; all of my customers and potential customers from throughout my territory and around the country were gathered in one place. I knew it was my big chance and I took full advantage. It was a time and money saver for me to be able to meet with clients from northern Maine and southwestern Rhode Island all in the same place with no driving and not having to lug sample cases in and out of the trunk of my car.

To me, trade shows and business fairs are like speed-dating parties. They bring a huge number of prospects to one place—which, to be honest, can be a potential jackpot or a scary and overwhelming circus. This section will put trade shows into perspective.

For certified businesses, numerous trade shows exist at the local and national level. If you wanted, you could probably attend a trade show or business expo every week. I recommend obtaining calendars of supplier diversity business fairs (and other events) through many sources, so you have a comprehensive list to review if you are considering participation. Also do the following:

- Visit WBENC's website, which shares information on its national events, including online registration for attendees, sponsors and exhibitors. You can also connect to the websites of each of our regional affiliates.
- Check corporate supplier diversity websites.

Networking

- Read supplier diversity industry magazines such as *MBE* (Minority Business Entrepreneur) *Magazine*, *Minority Business Insider*, *WE*, and *Enterprising Women*.
- Visit TradeNet (www.tradenet.gov), the US government's website trade show calendar, provided by the Department of Commerce.
- If you are a WBENC member, the monthly "President's Report" provides information on national and regional events
- Read e-zines available from websites such as www.SBTV.com, www.WomensCalendar.org, and www.WE-Inc.org provide calendars.

Yes, trade shows offer an amazing opportunity to meet corporate buyers face-to-face, but just like speed-dating parties, they are not for everyone at all times. You may want to visit trade shows as an attendee only to network and make face-to-face connections, or you may make exhibiting with a trade show booth a large component of your marketing plan. Here are the key issues to consider when making the decision on how to participate:

- **Do you have the budget to buy a booth, travel to the event, and cover accommodation expenses?** Booths can cost from several hundred to several thousand dollars, depending on the size and caliber of the event and the booth's design. Remember, this is not a retail show, so you will not be selling your products at your booth. You will only display enough information to entice corporate buyers to learn more about you. WBE Nancy Michaels has an alternative strategy. She uses Ziploc bags and items from a dollar store to put together "Trade Show Survival Kits." The day before the trade show, she pays the hotel concierge (on average, two dollars per room) to distribute the kits. The next day, she walks the trade-show floor and asks her prospects and customers if they got their survival kit.

- **Will your prospects be attending?** Business fairs list their corporate sponsors, exhibitors, and speakers on their websites, often months in advance, so you should be able to gather this information. Do not invest in a booth if your potential buyers are not attending. However, you may want to attend as a non-exhibitor to check out other MWBEs or make other networking contacts. If you want to get the advertising associated with a sponsorship level, barter with the organization to get a higher level of advertising exposure in exchange for giving up that booth space.
- **Will you have help staffing your booth?** Particularly for multiday business fairs, you will want an employee or other informed person to help staff your booth if you plan to walk around the event or attend seminars and meals. Most exhibitor fees include attendance for more than one representative of your company, so the additional cost is small compared to the opportunity offered. Cindy Tower says she brought just two additional staff to the first WBENC conference at which she exhibited but upped that to six the next year. She walks the trade-show floor along with the supplier diversity representative of a current client, who introduces her to his or her colleagues at targeted prospect companies. Two other employees walk the floor as well to ensure broad coverage with three more back at the booth.
- **Do you have a professional-looking booth?** Your professional image is extremely important at a trade show. As with your marketing materials, your trade show display (whether a full booth or a tabletop) must show that you are capable of playing in the big leagues. If you cannot do it right, do not do it. Also invest in a token giveaway that is branded with your corporate name and a phone number or website address. I use a specific tag with a catchy line. Recently, I purchased small screwdrivers from Julie Levi's Progressive Promotions. On the box, I put a label that reads, "Don't get screwed

Networking

on your next real-estate transaction." Small, useful giveaways keep your contact information in front of the corporate representative long after the trade show ends. Once you have invested in your booth, you will be able to amortize its cost across many events. Some businesses display their booths in the lobby area of their companies, providing an attractive alternative use.

When you do make the decision to exhibit at a supplier diversity trade show, here are tips from experienced MWBEs on how to work a trade show like a pro:

- **Find out who you want to see**—Again, research all exhibitors, sponsors, speakers, and other attendees. Find out which competitors, corporate buyers, association leaders, VIPs, and other good contacts will be attending. Know whom you want to target, where their booths or workshops are, and how you plan to approach them. This may mean crisscrossing the trade-show floor, but it will ensure that you have an opportunity to see your target firms.
- **Consider volunteering your time or expertise**—Contact the organizers to offer your products or services in exchange for an ad in the event program or other valuable exposure.
- **Organize an event within the event**—Office Depot conducts workshops at its conference booth. There is no reason you could not do the same—with permission and support of the sponsoring organization, of course.
- **Participate in silent auctions and raffles**—It can be worth the investment to bid on business-related offerings at a trade show's raffle. Many silent auctions nowadays feature the prize of "lunch with a CEO or CPO." This unique opportunity has proven more than worth the cost for such certified WBEs as Nancy Michaels, whose $1,050 bid for lunch with Office Depot's then CEO Bruce Nelson led to one of the largest contracts of her lifetime,

and it lasted for ten years. Donna Cole of Cole Chemical in Houston took this concept one step further: She bid $6,000 for lunch with the chief procurement officer of Shell. When their lunch date arrived, Donna, who has a passion for cooking, used herbs from her garden and made a spectacular Asian fusion lunch for the CPO and his managers. The Shell team toured Cole's headquarters and marveled at the wall murals depicting Asian, African, and Native American women in cultural dress going about their daily lives. The procurement officer not only appreciated the experience, but also learned an enormous amount about Cole Chemical. At the time, Cole was losing opportunities due to bundling and global contracts, and the visit helped Donna begin a dialogue to carve out strategic pieces of business for her WBE.

- **Network with other suppliers**—Do not focus all your attention on potential customers. Take time to meet business owners who supply your current customers and may be potential strategic partners. Trade shows can also be a great place to meet potential mastermind group members or to form barter relationships.
- **Attend workshops and meals**—It does not all happen on the trade show floor! Do not spend *all* of your time at your booth and don't always sit with your best friend. Some of the best connections are made in other settings, particularly during informal moments like breaks, unscheduled evenings, receptions, and continental breakfasts where seating is not assigned.
- **Collect business cards at your booth for a raffle**—Ideally, hold a raffle for one of your products. This is a great way to attract visitors to your booth and collect names for your mailing list at the same time. The winner, of course, gets to sample your product for free and will feel good about it. If you have a service rather than a product, consider giving away something like an iPad;

you will definitely increase the traffic to your booth and create a memorable experience.

- **Bring more than enough marketing materials**—Never run out. The trade-show website will give you a basic idea of the number of event attendees you can expect. Plus, little gimmicks like chocolates or, better yet, clever trinkets branded with your company name are great for drawing people into your booth. A tip on trinkets: give something that will really be used—and used often—by your prospects, such as pens, notepads, or magnets. Yoyos and such are cute, but most people give them to a child or throw them in the trash after a spin or two.
- **Follow up, follow up, follow up**—Diane McClelland, cofounder and president of Astra Women's Business Alliance, advises MWBEs always to follow up in a timely manner after meeting at an event. This shows that you are serious about making a real connection. Trade shows can be exhausting, so by all means take a day or two to recover. But then your first order of business is to pursue every lead made at a trade show. Make your investment worthwhile by thanking all guests at your booth, saying "Nice to meet you" to all new contacts and answering any questions posed to you by booth visitors.
- **Do not sit down, and do not stand behind a table**—I know it is tiring, but plan ahead and wear comfortable shoes. At the end of the WBENC business fair, I sometimes feel that I cannot stand for one minute longer. Tables create barriers between you and your prospects, and you project more energy standing than sitting.
- If you have your booth number ahead of time, print cards that you can distribute at networking events that direct people to your booth.
- Write to your prospects and current clients, inviting them to drop by.

Deals Done on the Spot at Trade Shows

Sorry to disappoint, but this seldom happens. Do not go to a trade show expecting a deal to be done on the spot. *Success* should be defined as getting a contact with whom you can follow up. If you attend a trade show thinking you are going to get That One Big Contract to save your company from bankruptcy, you may as well try to win the money in Vegas. While trade shows can reap huge rewards for your company in the long run, keep your short-term expectations in check.

Host Your Own Networking Events

Tired of traveling to events? Bring the networking to you. Consider celebrating a new-product launch or business anniversary with a gathering of your contacts. If you have an impressive office or warehouse, hold the event in your space, and offer tours to your attendees to educate them about your business capabilities. Even if some invitees do not attend, they will learn of your success through your invitations.

Michelle Boggs of McKinley Marketing Partners incorporates her own events throughout the year for clients and prospects. A former member of the WBENC Board of Directors and The Forum, she invited all forum and board members to a reception at her firm's distinctive office in Old Town Alexandria in conjunction with a quarterly meeting. Her impressive office space and her generosity are a good showcase for her company. The event was a big success and gave each of the attendees a more personal connection to Michelle and her business.

NETWORKING MISTAKES TO AVOID

Networking Follow-Up

No matter which associations you join and which events you choose to attend or host, networking is a marathon, not a sprint.

Networking

Follow-up and regular contact is essential to maintaining the contacts you work so hard to cultivate. It takes time to get to the finish line.

You will no doubt develop your own style of follow-up and communication based on your business size, industry, prospect list, and personality. Here are some tips—again, for you to pick and choose for yourself—on maintaining your connections:

- **Pick up a pen**—While we all love the ease and immediacy of e-mail, sometimes a handwritten note can do wonders for a business relationship. A "thank you," "nice to meet you," "thought this article would interest you," or other communication can brighten someone's day and show that you are a business owner willing to take a little extra time for your clients and friends. In today's Internet world, a personal, handwritten note is memorable.
- **Build a strong database**—Take the time to research and invest in the best database or contact management system you can afford. Popular choices include ACT, Microsoft Outlook, and FileMaker Pro. There are also many good, industry-specific customer-relationship management systems. Check with your trade association. It goes without saying that your primary list should include e-mail, addresses, and telephone numbers—all in one place and synced to your cellular phone. My iPhone is the most valuable tool I have found in the past ten years to help me communicate while I am on the road. I use the Dropbox app to keep copies of my primary documents, including the books and articles I am writing. Computerized databases are also essential these days for easy sorting, creating mailings, and keeping track of phone calls, e-mails, and meeting notes. Immediately update your database when you receive news of an address change so your list is always 100 percent current. As soon as I return from a business fair or conference, I have all my new contacts added to my database. Throughout the year, the first thing

I do every Monday morning is to go through the business cards I have collected over the prior week and enter them into my database.
- **Keep regular contact**—It is important to reach out to your entire database six or seven times a year a year to stay on everyone's radar screen. Have something interesting to say. Many people choose the December holiday season to send a mailing. Another option is to celebrate your business' anniversary each year with a card and perhaps a small gift. I like to send a Valentine to remind my customers how much I "love" them. One year I sent a heart-shaped key ring that said that they were the "key to my success." Recipients have taken the time to e-mail, call, or otherwise comment on the card. Black History Month, Women's History Month, and other dates can become your branded recognition opportunity.

The goal of all this networking and meeting and greeting and follow-up, not to mention the certification and marketing we have already explored, is to secure a meeting with a corporate purchasing executive at your top prospect company. Now that you have started to build and maintain your network of contacts, the next chapter begins your step-by-step guide to pitching for, winning, and keeping your dream contract.

CASE STUDY

RANJINI PODDAR, PRESIDENT, ARTECH INFORMATION SYSTEMS, LLC

Ranjini Poddar is an attorney by training, but after growing up helping in her family's small business and earning an undergraduate IT major, creating this workforce management company was not a stretch. The firm recently raised its $500 million revenue goal to $1 billion. Ranjini says, "When we were getting started in 1993, if someone had said we would be a $50 million company, I would have said 'Wow,' but last year we did $379 million and are approaching the half-million-dollar mark." The company is now the tenth-largest staffing company in the United States.

Ranjini adds, "We were unsure about how getting certified would affect our company but thought it might result in a competitive advantage in acquiring new business." The bet has paid off. While they already had a significant client base when they came to WBENC, new opportunities have arisen. The company has a well-thought-out plan for targeting new business development, and certification is just a part of the strategy.

Even the name of the company was a tactic for acquiring new clients. "We wanted a name that started at the beginning of the alphabet so that it would be at the top of vendor lists. And it worked; one of our first clients was the Port Authority of New York and New Jersey. We were an approved vendor but not doing any business. Someone told the buyer to call a particular company, but he could not remember the name. Ours was at the beginning of the list, so he called us instead."

Networking is another important part of the strategy. "I had met Rondu Vincent of Pfizer at various diversity events," Ranjini says. "We had been trying to get a contract with Pfizer for some time. At a WBENC event, I was able to introduce Rondu to Michael Robinson of IBM, a longtime Artech client. Michael was able to speak to Rondu regarding the services we had performed for IBM over the years. After his vetting process, Rondu fast-tracked us in terms of receiving an opportunity to support Pfizer. Today Artech is recognized as a top supplier by Pfizer. This would not have been possible without the networking opportunities presented by WBENC."

Ranjini believes that visibility at diversity and industry events is part of a long-term strategy that builds both her corporate and personal brand. "Sponsoring and exhibiting at major industry trade shows has been our most powerful marketing strategy as far as generating new business. I was the co-WBE chair for the 2009 WBENC National Conference in San Francisco. The best way to express my experience is by stating that, to this day, people still recognize me from the panel discussions.' Artech is also co-chairing the 2013 conference. The investment provides overall visibility and name recognition for me and the company. It is something you build on."

On an annual basis, Artech sponsors various national and local WBENC and NMSDC events together with industry events. "We focus on our target audience, gain tremendous visibility among them, and then follow up to close deals." Ranjini says. But she cautions, "It does not happen overnight. At Artech, we understand that meeting a representative of a potential new client is only the beginning. We must schedule our time accordingly, not only to identify additional decision makers but to determine the size and scope of the prospect's program and decided whether or not it is a good fit for Artech."

Artech has won numerous awards from industry associations as well as from corporate clients. According to Ranjini, "Awards build credibility when we are pitching a new company."

Chapter Five

Alternative and Advanced Supplier Strategies

As you continue to build relationships and begin to plan your official sales pitch to corporations, you should consider the various entry points that are available to you. While the most common scenario—and the strategy I have focused on thus far—is for one certified supplier to pursue a contract with one corporate buyer, there are several other possibilities. This chapter outlines a variety of alternative supplier strategies and how to make them work for you.

Why is it important to consider alternative strategies? A WBENC survey of its corporate members found that an average of only 38 percent of the spending of Fortune 1000 corporations is up for renewal or rebidding each year. Why? Think about trends in the business world today: the pressures of cost cutting, globalization, vendor consolidation, and bundled contracts (consolidating two or more procurement requirements for goods or services previously provided under separate, smaller contracts) have narrowed opportunities to attain new business for WBEs and other suppliers.

Smart business owners change with the times and do what they can to grow, even in a challenging economic environment. Dell's Cyndi Hopkins says, "As global supply-chain management evolves, WBEs must stay informed about current trends that impact corporate supply chains if they want to present themselves as sophisticated companies that can earn business and deliver results. Two trends we see impacting procurement today are globalization and building effective relationships.

Breaking Through

"Globalization of suppliers is key to meet the dynamic needs of new markets and the customers we serve," she says. "It is imperative that WBEs develop a global presence aligned with market growth opportunities for the corporations with which they want to do business."

Going global was a customer-focused tactic and advanced strategy for ASAP Solutions Group. Nancy Williams, its principal, says, "Our strategy has always been to look at challenging business issues with childlike eyes and strategize with our clients to see what can be, not what cannot be."

ASAP opened a division in India at the request of a client—Accenture—who asked for their help. Nancy says,

> Roz [her partner] and I are true entrepreneurs—we have faith that when we jump off the cliff, the parachute will open. How difficult can it be? We go off fearless, with the attitude "Let's make it happen." It came from Accenture saying, "We would like you to help us over there." The power is in not knowing, because if you truly understand the difficulties, it will scare the living hell out of you.
>
> We believe whatever we see as our future, we can achieve it. We feel that strongly about our team and our capability. As it turned out, when you go to India to open a business, it is not as difficult as individuals as it would be as a company. So that is what we did: we opened as individuals to get it done quickly. They also offered us a ten-year tax holiday. So we said to ourselves, "OK, we can go and invest and do it."
>
> We were smart and lucky. Our country head had worked for us for twelve years in the United States and went back to India to head up our operation. In compliance with country requirements, he became a nominal partner. Our success has also benefited from Roz finding and connecting with individuals that shared our core beliefs. To maintain quality, we do constant video conferencing, we bring people over to work here in the States, and we go there

and work with them. It started in response to Accenture's request, but now we work with a lot of clients there.

STRATEGIC ALLIANCES

For a variety of reasons, such as size, geographic location, or technological limitation, some MWBEs are not able to fulfill all requirements of a particular corporate contract. In such cases, a strategic alliance with another MWBE may be a smart strategy for pitching and winning the business. For our purposes, "strategic alliance" can be defined as a formal business relationship (short of a partnership, merger, or acquisition) formed for the purpose of fulfilling a corporate contract that each company could not fulfill on its own.

How exactly does this work? An alliance can comprise two, three, or several businesses related in the following ways:

- **Vertical integration**—For example, a graphic design firm could partner with a web hosting company to provide full web design and implementation services under one contract. That same graphic designer might partner with a printer whose quality and service matches their own corporate culture, thus providing a corporate client with end-to-end production of brochures and other paper products. Or all three could join together.
- **Horizontal integration**—You can partner with a competitor to increase geographic reach or staff capacity. Two technology staffing firms, for example, might unite to provide staffing in multiple cities rather than just their own. In this way, Company 1 can fulfill the needs of corporations that might be headquartered in that company's region, but that have locations in more than one area of the country that can be serviced by Company 2. Note: If you form a new company or partnership, remember to have that entity certified in its own right so that there will be no questions as to its ability to compete within the supplier diversity process.

CHEAT SHEET

How do you find companies interested in an alliance? This cheat sheet offers several strategies to try. Of course you will want to vet potential partners as you would any business partner, but one good sign that it is a viable, strong business is to look for its certification. Certification from a respected organization shows that the company has been carefully vetted. And if you meet a potential partner when you are out networking, you will know right away that the other businessperson understands marketing and networking just like you do.

FORMING A STRATEGIC ALLIANCE

- Attend events for MWBEs—It is important to show up at events that other successful certified businesses will attend.

- Advertise—Consider placing an ad in your industry newsletter, magazine, or website, or on Google or other search engines. Create a special Facebook page.

- Search—Search supplier databases such as WBENCLink for companies in the industry or geographic location in which you are looking to partner.

- Network with other businesses in your industry to learn who is well respected by your peers.

- Ask your current clients who they use in other regions of the country or for synergistic products and services.

- When you do form an alliance, promote it.

Alternative and Advanced Supplier Strategies

A great example of a creative alliance is Dell's Entrepreneur in Residence Initiative (EIR). The EIR gives the entrepreneurial community a direct conduit to the company and enables Dell to be more engaged in creating solutions that create, grow, and sustain this critical sector of US and global economies. Through the office of the EIR, Dell recently launched the Center for Entrepreneurs, a community designed by and for entrepreneurs. Ingrid Vanderveldt, Dell's first EIR, worked with Dell to launch the $100-million Dell Innovators Credit Fund to provide entrepreneurs with financial and technology resources they need to maximize their potential for innovation, speed to market, and job creation. It also helps eliminates the need for them to spend their equity capital on technology and instead help startups to preserve this for other business needs. You can keep up with this initiative at the official company blog: Direct2Dell.

Informal Referral Networks

If formal strategic alliances are not the right choice for you, you may want to consider an informal vendor-referral arrangement. As you will read in Camilla Sullivan's case study at the end of this chapter, "It is who knows you, not who you know." LinkedIn can be a wealth of referrals, as can your network on Facebook and Twitter. You can strategically utilize your social networks, especially LinkedIn, as a referral network.

SECOND-TIER OPPORTUNITIES

Second-tier suppliers are diverse suppliers used as subcontractors by a first-tier (also known as "prime") supplier to a corporation. Second-tier suppliers generally count toward a company's supplier diversity goals, so it is in a corporation's best interest to ensure that their larger first-tier suppliers meet and do business with smaller second-tier players, and that the first-tier suppliers report on their usage of diverse subcontractors. Second-tier supplying is yet another door into a corporation, and one that

Breaking Through

MWBEs are using increasingly. I strongly encourage you to consider second-tier opportunities in your quest to grow your business.

Consider this more detailed definition of second-tier supplying from Rutgers University:

"Second Tier is a function of who is the customer. A First Tier company is a supplier that invoices your company for goods and/or services rendered *directly* by that supplier. A Second Tier supplier is a supplier that invoices a company's First Tier supplier for goods and/or services rendered. The Second Tier process strongly encourages or requires its prime suppliers/contractors to develop a program that engages MWBE in its supply process and encourages the development of MWBE firms."[i]

Why are second-tier programs important to corporations and MWBEs? As Rutgers University states on its procurement website, "Second Tier sourcing programs have value because, by supporting the growth of minority- and woman-owned business on all levels of the economic food chain, they enhance the economic viability of all business concerns.

"The overall objective is to encourage the development and implement sustainable opportunities for [MWBE] to participate in the customer's procurement processes where it makes economic sense to do so.

Kelly Services, WBENC corporate member and 2013 Top Corporation for America's Women and Minority-owned Businesses, uses WBEs as second-tier on their contracts. At the 2013 award ceremony, Pamela Berklich, senior vice president of the Center of Excellence, said, "Investing in supplier development has been the key to our success. We hold supplier summits, conduct mentoring programs, present awards, and provide a professional development series. Our success relies on financially healthy and sustainable networks of talent search and HR

Alternative and Advanced Supplier Strategies

suppliers for our clients. SDI (Carmen Castillo) has been our number-one WBE partner. The first year they did $250,000 with Kelly and are now doing $21 million."

A section on the Wells Fargo supplier diversity website further describes the importance and benefits of second-tier programs:

> Wells Fargo Second Tier Suppliers are subcontractors hired by a Wells Fargo contracted supplier to provide goods and/or services under their Wells Fargo contract. This approach provides business opportunities for companies that may not qualify as a First Tier supplier. Gaining experience as a Second Tier supplier also helps build relationships with Wells Fargo which may lead to potential First Tier supplier opportunities in the future. Many of America's large corporations highly value Second Tier suppliers. They may be Second Tier, but they are by no means second-class.

In fact, some corporations require all first-tier suppliers to establish diverse spend goals with their subcontractors. For example, Bank of America provides a supplier diversity orientation with all first-tier suppliers once their contract is implemented, laying out the bank's expectations with respect to second-tier goals, certification of subcontractors, and second-tier reporting requirements. To prove its seriousness, Bank of America monitors these second-tier results quarterly.

A potential drawback to second-tier corporate supplying, however, is that the onus for creating opportunities and reporting results often falls on the first-tier supplier, whose programs are often not as developed or as well-monitored as Fortune 500 corporate supplier diversity programs. This means that you must remain diligent and remind your first-tier company to report your contribution to any contracts in which you participate. Remember, particularly if the first-tier supplier is not a MWBE, you are bringing enormous value as a diverse business. They need you.

The WPEO is working to correct this problem by creating a program that encourages corporate members to bring their First Tier suppliers to a meet and greet with WBEs. According to President Marsha Firestone, "This is an opportunity that the corporations support strongly because as contracting consolidation has decreased MWBE bidding opportunities, they have increased with second-tier requirements built into these contracts. Some of the larger WBE companies are first-tier and have their own diversity spend requirements in their contracts."

Now in its second year, both WPEO-NY and WPEO-DC have implemented the program. As well allowing WBEs to learn of subcontracting opportunities, the first-tier companies are happy to learn of the program and gain access to these certified businesses that can assist them with carrying out the diversity requirements of their own contracts. At recent events, a few examples include Colgate brought Young & Rubican, Major League Baseball brought Supplier Gateway, Merck brought Fisher Scientific, Pitney Bowes brought Firmenich, and Johnson & Johnson brought Omnicon, who later joined the WPEO as a corporate member to gain more regular interaction with WBEs in the program.

Sometimes a larger WBE is the first-tier company, as illustrated by Deutsche Bank bringing cSubs. cSubs CEO Julie Auslander says, "I don't ever forget how blessed I am to be in the top half of 1 percent of WBE businesses that have the critical mass to be a First Tier supplier to Fortune 500 companies. With these blessings comes a responsibility to pay it forward and live in gratitude for what we have. As proud as I am of our Done Deals as a WBE to Sponsor companies, numbering 2,467 last year, I am even more proud of cSubs Done Deals WBE to WBE, numbering eighteen. This means that eighteen second-tier WBE companies have been mentored and were able to service Fortune 500 companies by doing business with cSubs."

Alternative and Advanced Supplier Strategies

In just the last year, largely attributable to this program, WPEO's Done Deals have grown from eight thousand to 18,000.

How can you make your second-tier status known to the corporation receiving the benefit of your services? One suggestion is to offer to help the first-tier supplier complete the paperwork reporting required by a corporation. Another tactic, as suggested by Heather Herndon Wright, whose additional suggestions appear in the Cheat Sheet below, is to offer to accompany your first-tier supplier on sales calls. This ensures that the corporation knows a MWBE is involved in the contract, and it helps you build a relationship with the end user.

CHEAT SHEET

To become a second-tier supplier, you will need to implement many of the same marketing and networking strategies you have been using to reach corporate buyers. Heather Herndon Wright has been involved in every aspect of WBENC—Executive Director of an RPO, WBE, WBENC staff, WBENC board, and corporate member. She offers these specific pointers from her experience on both sides of the table—as corporate supply chain director and as a WBE.

HOW TO BECOME A SECOND-TIER SUPPLIER

- Never bypass the chance to perform at a second-tier level if it is suggested to you by your supplier diversity contacts. You are not giving up your relationship with your customer; you are just serving his or her needs in a different way.

- Remember that corporate buyers are often very busy and overwhelmed, so they are not always thinking about where you might fit in their supply chain. You need to come to them with out-of-the-box solutions. Educate your customers on exactly what you can provide, and work with them to identify multiple points of entry into their supply chain so you can operate most effectively.

- Actively market yourself as a second-tier supplier as part of your pitch to corporations. Immediately look for indirect ways to supply them in any capacity you can. This is particularly important in today's environment of outsourced procurement or when a corporation is seeking a global, multiproduct contract. Can your business fulfill a particular regional need or supply a niche product?

- Do not be afraid to market yourself to your competitors. Larger competitors may be able to include your business as a second-tier supplier in a large contract with an existing customer. In addition, this could result in a great way for you to expand your customer base and supply your products or services to additional companies already being served by your competitor.

- Show your value to the first-tier suppliers. If you are a reliable, high-quality second-tier supplier, chances are the Prime will partner with you again on other contracts.

- Do not stop at second -tier—look at third, fourth,

Alternative and Advanced Supplier Strategies

> and on down the line. There may be several points of entry for various product and service offerings in a single contract.
>
> - View your second-tier status as an opportunity to be mentored by the first-tier company. As a second-tier supplier, you are gaining experience to provide more value as a prime supplier.

While we are on the subject of second-tier supplying: Do you have a supplier diversity program for your company? If not, you should. No matter at what point you enter the supply chain, your diversity dollars not only help your customer's reporting needs and goals, but also increase your own credibility. Furthermore, you can use your own diversity initiative as a marketing tool when you approach that corporate buyer or first-tier company.

Cathi Coan of Techway Services (see the case study in chapter seven) has growing relationships with other WBE firms: "Everything today is about partnerships. I met Keeli Jernigan from Trans-Expedite at a WBCS event. We work with her to provide reverse logistics to return used electronics. Anything that needs to be brought back from a company and shipped to our facility is handled by Trans-Expedite. They go in, pack it up, and ship to our facility. They have various warehouse facilities across the country. In Dallas we lease space from them. We are planning to co-locate and lease space at her other locations."

The partnerships do not stop there. "Recently, we were fortunate to be awarded a major contract with a health-care general purchasing office that represents 16,000 hospitals. Our technicians go on-site to do a data wipe on hard drives before obsolete equipment leaves the facility, which protects very sensitive data often protected by HIPAA regulations. Currently, we do not have the capability to take a large volume of calls from 16,000 hospitals, so we outsourced to Westpark

Communications, a sister WBE. I met Kathie Edwards at a Summit and Salute event, and we became a teaming partner."

Leslie Saunders of Leslie Saunders Insurance and Marketing derives an extraordinary 50 percent of her business from other WBEs. In turn, she uses other WBEs as suppliers. "My broker for my employee benefits is a WBE," she says. "And I have a woman attorney, and my trade show booth was made by a WBENC member, as were my holiday cards, my promotional materials, and so on. Whenever possible, I use a supplier from WBENC. When we work with each other, good things happen. I think that there are a lot of opportunities for WBENC businesses to do business with each other."

BECOME A BUSINESS SOLUTION PARTNER

- Corporations are always on the lookout for seamless service, and one way for smaller MWBEs to break into the supply chain is to make it their business to package the skills, products, or logistics of several other companies. By integrating an entire solution and offering several services in one package, you make life easier for a corporate buyer who does not want twenty relationships requiring twenty invoices and twenty phone calls a day.
- Patty Klein, CEO of A-Plus Meetings & Incentives, says, "We are your one point of contact for travel, production, AV, décor, food and beverage, offsite events, and more, including cutting-edge technologies like mobile applications. For production, we have internal graphic-arts capabilities plus writers for materials. For videos or more-complex materials, we contract out to appropriate suppliers for each program. For example, for a thousand-person program for WBENC, we manage separate vendors for video production, scenic design, printed invitations/show books, preproduction of PowerPoint presentations, and onsite management of the show and AVP. For the video production, we are on site for taping and guide the editing process."

Alternative and Advanced Supplier Strategies

SUCCESS STORY

BILLIE BRYANT, PRESIDENT AND CEO, CESCO

Billie Bryant, the first Forum chair and former WBENC board member, has an incredible success story of winning contracts through subcontracting. It demonstrates the values of patience and building relationships to achieve big results. Always seeking new business, Billie became aware of two large, bundled RFPs from the Dallas Independent School District (DISD)—one for office supplies and the other for office equipment, with some consulting services included. She knew that her company could participate in both RFPs by partnering with larger corporations. Her door to opportunity involved promoting herself as a second-tier supplier whose WBE status could help larger companies win the contracts.

Billie decided to contact the DISD to educate them on the utilization of WBEs and the importance of the district supporting local businesses. It did not hurt that Billie could say that her business and her home both supported the district in taxes each year and that she had graduated three sons from the Dallas school system. (Indeed, this is a good lesson in using what you've got.)

Billie visited DISD to share a presentation on supplier diversity, educating them on the value of her small business in partnership with any large supplier. Next she called some of the large companies that attended the pre-bid meeting to sell her services. According to Billie, it is very important that large companies understand all the value-added services that a small business can bring to a large, bundled contract. It is also very important that technology be among those value-added skills. On the supply side of the RFP, Billie eventually formed an alliance with Office Depot and Corporate Express.

To address the equipment proposal, she had an existing partnership with Xerox dealing with major corporations in facilities management and equipment. However, one of her main contacts at Xerox, Tracey

Breaking Through

Whitaker, had since retired and was working for Kinkos. When Tracey evaluated the DISD RFP for Kinkos, he remembered working with CESCO and contacted Billie for a potential strategic alliance. Tracey pulled together a team including a few MWBEs, and the group won the business. As you can see, strong relationships last even when supplier diversity professionals change companies.

In the end, the DISD director of purchasing thanked Billie for educating the district on how smaller MWBE businesses can work with large suppliers, and Billie realized her goal of participating in both large, bundled contracts. Billie used her commitment, contacts, and hard work to form valuable alliances to service large customers.

MATCHMAKER, MATCHMAKER, MAKE ME A MATCH

Is your head spinning yet? I know it can be overwhelming to consider all the options from prime contracts to strategic alliances to second-, third- and fourth-tier supplier relationships. Sometimes certified businesses can feel like they have too many decisions to make. This, again, is where the supplier diversity community—certification organizations in particular—demonstrates its true commitment to your success and the success you can bring to America's corporations.

Enter matchmaking.

WBENC, our partner organizations, and our corporate members provide connecting resources to help you find the right fit with the right partners for your business. For example, our MatchMaker Meeting Series connects WBENC-certified WBEs with corporate purchasing officials for private, face-to-face meetings to discuss potential opportunities.

Women Business Enterprises apply to attend these meetings by completing a "WBE Profile Sheet" and application attached to the notification e-mail for each specific MatchMaker meeting in which

Alternative and Advanced Supplier Strategies

they wish to participate. These forms are then used by the MatchMaker corporation's purchasing personnel, along with a supplier's WBENCLink profile, in the selection process. (This is yet another reason to make sure your WBENC profile—and any online profile—is always current.) Attendees are then selected for this valuable opportunity to meet with corporations that have *preselected* them.

CHEAT SHEET

While matchmaker programs can vary from organization to organization, the program time line for a WBENC MatchMaker event provides insight into how the process works:

> ### *WBENC MATCHMAKER MEETING PROGRAM TIME LINE*
>
> **Stated Goal**
>
> The goal of the MatchMaker Program is to pair WBENC-certified women business enterprises (WBEs) and corporate and government purchasing officials for private, one-on-one meetings to discuss business opportunities.
>
> Each corporation participating in a MatchMaker event works differently, and the structure of the event varies, so we tailor a schedule to meet a corporation's individual needs.
>
> **Eight Weeks Out**
>
> WBEs receive announcement via matchmaker@wbenc.org, WBENC's e-mail dedicated to managing MatchMaker and sourcing opportunities.

Seven Weeks Out

Reminder notices are sent. WBEs are encouraged to submit their profiles as early as possible. WBENC vets WBE applications to confirm that the WBE is certified with WBENC and may do additional screening per the agreement with the corporation (location of business in a specific geographic region, and so on).

Six Weeks Out

Deadline for submission of WBE profiles for those interested in participating in the MatchMaker event.

Corporation or government agency begins review of profiles and selection of WBEs.

Four Weeks Out

Selected WBEs are sent notice about their participation in the MatchMaker meeting. Corporation must notify WBENC of nonbuyer appointments, such as appointments with supplier diversity managers. This information is passed along to the WBE selected.

Three Weeks Out

Final notices sent to WBEs selected to participate in the program. WBEs not selected for the MatchMaker are also notified. While it is not always possible, due to the length of a corporation's decision-making process, we strive to

Alternative and Advanced Supplier Strategies

> provide a minimum of three weeks' notice so that WBEs can get the best possible rate for their travel and hotel accommodations.
>
> **Two Weeks Out**
>
> Deadline for selected WBEs to confirm their availability to participate in the MatchMaker meeting. Appointment times are scheduled with specific corporate representative(s) and WBE. Confirmation e-mails with specifics on the event and appointment times are sent to the selected WBEs.

Are matchmaker meetings for everyone? As with any other business opportunity, conduct a cost-benefit analysis to make certain that this is an appropriate opportunity for you and your business. While there is no fee to participate in a MatchMaker meeting, you will be responsible for covering all your costs for travel and any other expenses you incur.

MAKING THE MOST OF A MATCHMAKER MEETING

The advanced strategy of matchmaker meetings is a serious endeavor. You must be thoroughly prepared for both the meeting itself and the doors it might open quickly. Here are some important tips:

- Be prepared before you get on the plane; make certain that all your materials are current and that you are in a position to fulfill any contract you may be discussing. Even though a matchmaker meeting is not a formal presentation, you should develop presentation materials that tell your company's story and that can be left behind with the corporate representative.

Breaking Through

- Find out beforehand how much time will be allotted to each meeting, and craft your pitch accordingly. Do not start a one-hour presentation if you have only twenty minutes. (See the next chapter for more suggestions on planning and executing your sales pitch.)
- Take the time to attend the meeting yourself, even if your vice president of business development normally makes new business calls. Your presence adds weight.
- Be on time. There is never an excuse for tardiness.
- Show up if you scheduled an appointment. At a recent WBENC MatchMaker, two WBE firms that had been selected to participate didn't show up or even call. They will *never* have the opportunity to do business with the corporation or to participate in another WBENC MatchMaker. Do not apply if you do not plan to attend.
- While corporations make every effort to make certain you are matched with the correct person in the company, do your own research and evaluate the specific opportunity with your own cost-benefit analysis. Do not be afraid to ask if there is someone else you might meet with while you are in town.
- Manage your expectations. View the meeting as the beginning of a relationship, not an all-or-nothing event.
- To maximize your time, try to schedule meetings with other current or potential clients in the geographic location where you are attending a matchmaker meeting.
- Follow up with a thank-you letter and additional information, no matter the result of the one-on-one meeting. At the very least, a matchmaker meeting is a great way to make a new connection in a prospect corporation.

WBE Mercedes LaPorta, president of Mercedes Electric Supply, Inc., has certainly made the most of the MatchMaker opportunities she has received through WBENC over the years. In preparation for the 2005 WBENC national conference in Las Vegas, Mercedes

Alternative and Advanced Supplier Strategies

requested a MatchMaker meeting with MGM Properties. She says, "I was able to meet with the head of the diversity department at the MatchMaker meeting, but also, thanks to WBENC's help, set up a couple of meetings with the buyers beforehand—for MGM's properties New York-New York and Treasure Island."

Mercedes used her MatchMaker opportunity to demonstrate her capabilities and relevant experience to MGM: "When I had my meeting, I had my company information with me and explained what exactly it is that I have done. I have supplied the electric materials for the Ritz Carlton in Key Biscayne and for the JW Marriott in Miami. This showed that I was familiar with hotels and the electric materials they would need to buy. I had a portfolio of twenty-seven years of projects. I also demonstrated the fact that I had been doing business on a national level before, with Office Depot. I was also able to relay to them that I had done a project in Las Vegas. They got a pretty good view [of my ability to handle their business]."

After the success of the MatchMaker meeting, Mercedes followed up with her diversity contact, who put her in touch with MGM's construction department. Mercedes Electric has since started to do business with New York-New York, MGM Mirage, and the MGM Grand in Las Vegas.

The US Small Business Administration also conducts a series of business matchmaking conferences throughout the United States in conjunction with the US Chamber of Commerce. (Visit www.sba.gov for information on this and other one-on-one opportunities presented at these events.) The SBA program offers multiple appointments with representatives of both the private sector and government agencies. An online registration system puts you in the driver's seat to determine which agencies and companies you are targeting, but the downside of this arrangement is that the companies and agencies have not preselected you (as they do with WBENC's MatchMaker series), so there may not be a match. They also provide several webinars that can help prepare you for their and other matchmaker events. Honest evaluation of your research is a key to a successful event for you and your company. To find more matchmaker opportunities, research additional associations and organizations.

Here is what happened to Judy Bradt, CEO of Summit Insight.

> My business development time is limited, so I focus on supplier diversity conferences that are the right fit. I applied to the US Small Business Administration's Business Matchmaking event in May of 2012 and was matched with Rudy Watley, chief of the Smithsonian Institution's Supplier Diversity program. Before I went, I tailored my capability statement to focus on the expertise I had that might be useful to his programs, and I prepared questions for him about the biggest challenges he faces in serving small business.
>
> We really got along well and had a great first meeting. He thought it would be worth having a follow-up visit in his office, but said he wouldn't have time for that until after the Fourth of July. We set a date to follow up then.
>
> When I met with Mr. Watley and his assistant, Jennifer Chen, I had more detailed questions for him—about his needs, his budget, and his decision time frame. I suggested some ideas that could help, and he liked those. He told me his sole-source threshold was $8,500, and he wanted to know what I could do for him within that budget. He then asked me to write up my ideas into a short statement of work and e-mail those to him.
>
> I got in touch with my partners and reviewed costs to make sure the project would be profitable. We set another follow-up date for late August, when the person who could approve the project could review the proposal. Again, more follow up, as the September purchasing deadline got closer, but my

Alternative and Advanced Supplier Strategies

persistence was rewarded. On September 5, I signed a purchase order for my first contract with the Smithsonian Institution, to make recommendations for improving their Supplier Diversity website.

I hope this chapter has opened your eyes to the many possible doors through which you can gain access to corporate contracts. Now that you know your audience (or audiences), it's time get out there and show your stuff. Get ready for your big pitch.

CASE STUDY

CAMILLA SULLIVAN, PRINCIPAL, VISIONISTA

Camilla Sullivan was pursuing a corporate career in her native Australia when her company, EDS, transferred her to Washington, DC, in 2005. In 2007 Camilla, frustrated with the corporate track, decided to become an entrepreneur and create the type of agency she had always wanted to hire when she was running marketing departments for major corporations. "I was tired of being a job description. From a professional perspective in delivering value to my company, I was frustrated with the agencies that bid on our work on the storytelling side when creating video and content. It was hard to get an agency to listen without their charging what amounted to highway robbery."

Getting started was not difficult for Camilla, who had a broad network of colleagues and friends familiar with her and with the quality of her work.

> I was introduced to someone who introduced me to someone. My first contract was supposed to be a small communications project and ended up as a massive branding campaign for Better Homes and Gardens Real Estate that was launching Realogy (Meredith Corporation). I picked up other clients as I

went along. The first clients all came from referrals. It is not who you know but who knows you. People that I worked with in previous lives started calling and saying, "I have a project." I built the business from there.

I found out about certification and thought "That is a great idea!" That was in 2010. I believed it to be a good way to open doors. Because of my background and network, we are really geared to Fortune 100 businesses, so WBENC is a good gateway for us. I was blown away when I met the WBENC community. Sometimes your feel alone as a leader. I went from a giant company to my own business. At WBENC events, I started meeting amazing women and got so much support it gave me the motivation to keep going.

Visionista has certainly taken off. Camilla reports, "Our commercials have been on national television. WBENC is an important client as well. We produce the Stars video for WBENC's Summit and Salute as well as video content for the website. Recently, we were fortunate that Procter & Gamble gave us an opportunity to create Eukanuba's—their new dog food—first national sixty-second commercial. Today we have begun a journey with AT&T to produce a diversity procurement video series that will be on their website. It gets more hits than many TV channels."

Every day brings new opportunities for Camilla. "We have a lot in the hopper and are building our pipeline. WBENC continues to help open doors for us. The more good work we do, the more work comes our way. As an entrepreneur, I have discovered there are no limits. I get to use all my credentials." Those credentials are impressive and include a marketing degree, an MBA, and a design degree, in addition to photography studies. Camilla even had the opportunity when working for Bearing Point to lecture at Yale.

The agency has grown and is one of those women-owned businesses now helping to rebuild the US economy. It has ten full-time employees, and Camilla notes, "We top that up with freelancers. Our crews are mostly local, as we work all over the country and we bring in key people as needed." The growth is not likely to be stalled, as Visionista is gaining recognition in their industry. In 2012, they were the recipient of two Stevie awards—one gold and one silver. Other awards include Hermes Creative Awards, Telly Awards, and Ava Awards.

Camilla has recently branched out to film production. Her Wall Street-focused documentary, *Ghost Exchange*, for which she is writer, producer, and director has received considerable buzz in the financial media, including the *Wall Street Journal*.

Chapter Six

The First P of Supplier Diversity Success: PREPARATION for the Big Meeting and Beyond

In the previous chapters you identified potential corporate customers, honed your marketing messages, and networked your way to relationships with supplier diversity professionals and potential strategic partners. You may even have experienced a one-on-one matchmaker meeting with a supplier diversity executive from a prospect company. Now it is time to prepare to take your message beyond the supplier diversity department and directly to the division of the company you will supply.

Remember that supplier diversity professionals—the primary targets of your attention thus far—do not usually make purchasing decisions. In many companies, they exercise a strong influence on the process. In some companies, all final contracts must have the sign-off of the supplier diversity executive, but that person is not the only decision maker.

This chapter helps you identify the decision makers for your particular product or service then advises you on the important topics of pricing and technology, both of which will be crucial to your ultimate pitch. For our purposes in this chapter, we will focus on making one pitch to one company, although it is likely you will be pursuing business with more than one company at a time.

Update Your Data

In chapter three, you learned the fundamental marketing strategy of registering with the supplier databases of all potential corporate customers. If you have not done this already, you must make sure not only that you are registered in the supplier database of the company you are actively pursuing, but also that your file is completely up-to-date. Various decision makers may look up your file, so be sure the information they find is current, persuasively presented, and accurate.

In addition to checking your profile in the corporation's database, take time now to make sure that your company website is up-to-date and fully functional. (Now is the time to replace any "Coming Soon!" pages with actual content.) Your live presentation is only one step in the pitch process; corporate executives may look for information about you and your business in a variety of places when they are assessing you.

Find Out Who Makes the Decisions

When you have a carefully developed relationship with your supplier diversity contact, he or she will likely introduce you to the proper office within the company. All you will need to do is ask for an introduction to the purchaser (or purchasers) you want to meet. (If you feel you do not have strong support from a corporate supplier diversity professional, go back to chapters three and four, or contact your regional partner organization or other MWBE organization for support and guidance.)

Corporations have various ways of contracting for goods and services, so you are likely to be directed to one of four places:

Formal Corporate Procurement RFP (Request for Proposal) Process: Formal, competitive sourcing processes are common for large-scale goods and services such as industrial equipment, technology purchases, and construction projects. For some firms, all commodities and services are purchased through RFPs, but the company may also perform a "sources sought" or "request for information" to develop lists of potential suppliers. As mentioned above, you must completely fill out the online or paper database questionnaire to even get into the game.

Kathy Mazon, senior business development leader of supplier diversity for Target, says, "As one aspect of Target's commitment to diversity and inclusion, we look to strategically integrate diverse suppliers into opportunities enterprise wide. It's essential that WBEs and all potential suppliers understand that the ability to adapt to existing supply-chain process requirements and technologies is critical. When participating in the RFx [RFPs, RFIs, RFQs] process, capabilities that are specific to the defined requirements should be directly addressed. If an award is received, it's the savvy business owner that continues collaboration with supplier diversity teams; this helps to position them for additional growth."

You will need to respond to the RFP with a formal written proposal, price quotes, and other requested information. As a certified business, take full advantage of your advocate in the supplier diversity department, who can advise you on the preparation of your proposal. That may prove to be the deciding factor in winning the contract. Everyone likes to be part of a winning team. If you can enlist the supplier diversity executive as a member of your team, you will help to make certain that your response is given appropriate consideration.

All companies exercise "due diligence" on RFP responses to make certain your business has the capacity to deliver on time and in budget. The larger the opportunity, the more information about your business, its finances, and its reputation (through references) will be required. Make certain your company's documentation is in good shape and complete when you respond

Planning

to an RFP. Your proposal might not be considered if it is incomplete.

You might deal with one of the following:

- **Commodity manager**—Large manufacturers, such as those in the automotive industry, utilize purchasing specialists who are expert in a narrow area. This system can expedite your identification of the correct "buyer," but may limit the creative inclusion of your product elsewhere in the company. Do not be afraid to ask for a referral to another commodity manager if you believe there is an opportunity elsewhere in the same corporation. Remember to do thorough research including the corporate website, annual reports, and SEC filings. You may have found from networking within your trade association that you can identify commodity managers specific to your industry.

    As discussed in chapter five, you should also ask if a referral to an existing prime supplier would be a good strategy for you and your business at this point. Recently, I was speaking with a senior executive of an Asian-owned business who informed me that the company had just landed a $1 billion, three-year contract with IBM. Part of their challenge in complying with the contract requirements was that they needed to identify diverse subcontractors within their commodity area for their second-tier goals. WBENCLink is a good place to start the search. Asking the executive director of the RPO is another good way to get a referral.

- **Central purchasing office**—Everyday business materials used by several departments in a corporation, such as office supplies, printing, furniture, and paper, are often procured through central buying offices. Generally, the corporation will enter multiyear contracts for a bundle of products or services—a great opportunity for strategic alliances or

168

second-tier. Each company is different, so research whether your product or service—be it rubber bands or human resources—is purchased department by department or through a central purchasing group.
- **Decentralized purchasing**—In addition to the more formal buying decisions mentioned above (and depending on corporate policy), departmental managers may be individual employees who are responsible for purchasing decisions that will affect only their department or regional office. Frequently, there will be a dollar cap on such authority. Note that many corporations switch back and forth between centralized purchasing and decentralized purchasing, so keep your research up-to-date. Do not assume that when your current contract expires you will be negotiating with the same official you dealt with last time around. Locally based purchasers generally procure such things as staffing services, trainers, local caterers, and printers, but each company is different, so *do your research*.

SECURE A MEETING WITH DECISION MAKERS

Whether you are interested in a first- or second-tier opportunity, you need to follow a logical, well-thought-out process to obtain a meeting with the decision maker who is open to your sales pitch. Just follow this simple who, when, what, and where strategy.

- **Who**—As mentioned above, work with your corporate supplier diversity contact to set up a meeting with the key decision maker(s) effecting procurement of your product or service. At every stage of the process, keep your supplier diversity contact in the loop. Never "go around" your original contact at a company. If you step on toes, you may risk losing not only this deal, but future opportunities.

When you do arrange a meeting with the decision maker, call your original contact a few days ahead of time to reconfirm exactly who will be in the room. Try to obtain the title and bio for each person so you will be fully prepared. Ideally, your supplier diversity contact will provide the bios, or you can search the company website, Google, or LinkedIn for information. The more you know about the people you are pitching (areas of expertise, associations they belong to, previous organizations they have worked for), the better you can form a personal connection during your pitch.

Also consider who will be on your side of the table. Will you bring staff? Strategic partners? I do not advise arriving with an entourage, but a few key staff members may be appropriate, depending on the size and complexity of the contract you are pursuing. Always inform the corporation of how many people will be attending, so they are not caught by surprise when you do not arrive alone.

- **When**—You need to set up your meetings according to the purchasing timetable of the company, which, unfortunately, does not always match your desired time frame. Again, work with your supplier diversity or RPO connections to determine the best time of year to make your pitch.

   When considering timing for your pitch, think carefully about your capabilities. You must go into the pitch fully capable of managing any work that may arise from the meeting. I cannot overemphasize the danger of overpromising. If you do not feel adequately prepared to fulfill a corporate contract if you receive one, do not set up a meeting that might result in work.

- **What**—Call and speak about expectations for the meeting with the decision makers with whom you will meet. Working with your supplier diversity contact, determine how much time you will have to make your presentation and how much information the meeting attendees will be expecting. You should certainly prepare for any possibility, but it is always helpful to have realistic expectations for what will be accomplished in the meeting and how long you will have to present. It is always

better to err on the side of gathering too much information than too little.
- **Where**—It is most likely you will need to travel to the location of the corporate decision maker. Include this time and cost in your planning.

CAREFULLY CONSIDER YOUR PRICING

When I was a manufacturers' representative, I sold to several different types of customers from small neighborhood shops to multistore chains to mass merchandisers. Pricing was based on the number of locations and the size of each order. Similarly, when you are supplying to corporations or prime contractors, your pricing will need adjusting, so be prepared to negotiate down. If you are doing business with the federal government, you are required by law and regulation to provide your best pricing.

While you are certainly the expert on the pricing of your products or services, keep in mind the following factors when preparing to discuss price with a potential corporate buyer:

First and foremost, understand what it takes for you to make a profit while you are expanding your market. There is absolutely no point selling to any new customer if you are going to lose money doing so. If you are Walmart, you can afford the occasional loss leader to get people into your store, but smaller companies (and pretty much everyone is smaller than Walmart) cannot afford to do business at a loss. Sometimes you have to "fire" your customer.

You should have a very clear understanding of your price structure and the marginal benefit you accrue from your own suppliers in servicing larger-quantity orders, so that you will know exactly how low you can go in a contract negotiation before you ever set foot in the door to pitch a corporation. Be conservative in your budgeting, and I highly recommend meeting with your accountant or financial manager before discussing price with any corporate buyer. Remember Cindy Tower's understanding the

Planning

"gigabyte" cost of providing document review? Her unique strategy provides a competitive advantage in the marketplace and predictable pricing for her client.

Be aware of the standards in your industry. Do as much research as you can (through networking, industry associations, and conversations with your supplier diversity contacts) to make sure you are in the same ballpark—or even lower priced—than your competition.

If you charge more than your competitors, be prepared to explain why. For instance, do you have newer or proprietary technology or do you offer different quantities?

Think about how time consuming it will be to work with this particular client. For both service and product-based businesses, high-maintenance clients can eat up your time and your staff's time, and as we all know, time is money. If possible, speak to a company's current suppliers to (tactfully) assess how demanding a client they may be; then set your prices accordingly.

Consider new ways to cut your costs or improve your cash flow to pass the savings on to your corporate customer. You might think about offering a discount if the customer pays an invoice within ten days, requiring custom orders to be paid up front, or even moving your warehousing closer to the customer to save on trucking costs. Again, look to the standards in your industry for discounting and cost-cutting ideas.

Service businesses should also consider implementing quantity discounts. Think about it: If your corporate customer is going to buy one hundred times the number of hours that your sales training company normally provides per customer, consider the fact that you will now have lower marketing costs because you are doing business with one customer rather than one hundred separate customers. There is also only one company to bill and one invoice to send. You benefit from the bulk sale as much as your customer, because you save on these costs and others. So you can (and should) pass this savings on to your customer as part of your contract negotiation.

For more help planning your pricing strategy, consult your professional association for comparative information about your particular field.

EVERYTHING YOU NEED TO KNOW ABOUT TECHNOLOGY...BUT WERE TOO BUSY CHECKING YOUR E-MAIL TO ASK

Nothing has changed more in the decade since I wrote the first edition of this book than technology. When we launched WBENC in 1997, we had to beg the RPOs to insist on requiring their WBE applicants to use an online application. Many businesses were not even computer literate at that time, and the RPO had to take the handwritten or typed application (remember typewriters?) and enter the data into the WBENC system. I had my very first cell phone in 1997, which worked in major cities only and went into roaming mode when I crossed the street from my office.

In today's fast-moving, competitive, global economy, technology plays a key role in any business relationship, and therefore will be addressed in any serious discussion about working with a large corporation. It is essential that you are prepared for the technological aspect of supplying corporate America, particularly as you prepare to make your sales pitch to decision makers.

As you read through the following advice, view technology knowledge and execution as marketing tools, competitive advantages, and essential costs of doing business. The technological aspect of servicing corporate America can be very challenging and potentially expensive, but the investment of time, energy, and resources is worth the reward.

Planning

Patty Klein of A-Plus Meetings & Incentives has used technology solutions to differentiate her very successful company from the pack. Among their offerings:

- Before the program
    - Smartphone-based registration website or app with agendas and hotel information
    - Social networking page(s) for pre-program discussions, both for business and social purposes
    - QR code to access site(s) and materials
- During the program
    - App with agendas, maps, locations, dress, and attendee lists
    - Calendar reminders for VIPs for key times (rehearsals, speeches, and so on)
    - Web/text/Twitter audience response system
    - Twitter screen updated during presentations
        - Comments about the presentation
        - Questions to the speaker, moderated or not
        - Chats between attendees
    - Instant speaker/session feedback and real-time agenda enhancements
    - Paperless conference (cloud-based materials distribution) delivers eco benefits
    - E-mail mobile boarding passes (airline permitting)
- After the program
    - Smartphone surveys
    - Continued social networking/updates on key program outcomes

Specific requirements vary widely depending on your industry, the company you are pitching, the amount of business you will be contracting for, and the complexity of your product or service. Therefore, for this section I have gathered recommendations from a diverse group of MWBEs, consultants, and corporate executives on the technology topics most frequently discussed.

Ten Technology Tips

Technology Tip #1: Technology is essential to servicing corporate America.

Technology cannot be avoided, so you may as well learn to love it. I certainly have. I thought I was really an early adapter when I carried the entire draft of this book on a tiny "jump drive" (also known as a thumb drive) that hung from my keychain and plugs into the USB port of my computer. Now I use cloud computing. I have Dropbox on my home and office computers as well as my iPad and iPhone and can access my book drafts and other critical documents anywhere. Furthermore, I can send a link to files too large to e-mail. I keep my boarding passes on my iPhone as well and even pay for my Starbucks with an app on my phone. When I sell my books at events, my customers can use my Square account to charge their purchase.

In many ways, technology is actually easier and more accessible to each of us than it was ten years ago. But your corporate technology needs are another matter altogether.

If you are still uncomfortable with technology, remember that, no matter what your age or interest level, technology is not something to be feared. If you feel uncomfortable, sign up for a continuing education class or hire an IT consultant to show you the ropes. WBE Pamela Chambers O'Rourke, president and CEO of Icon Information Consultants, LP, reminds beginners that you do not need to know how to install, run, and fix every software program on the market, but you do need to understand the basics for your industry.

So, just as you would not enter a meeting with a potential client without an understanding of the core financials of your business, do not enter a meeting without knowing—and being able to discuss—your company's technological capabilities. It is equally important to know the client's business and technology needs.

Corporate supplier diversity executives say the most important point for MWBEs regarding technology is to understand and adapt to the way in which large corporations and those companies in your industry do business through technology. From basic e-mail to sophisticated Customer Relationship Management (CRM) software, electronic enablement (e-enablement) is driven by a corporation's never-ending need for efficiency, quality, and economy. Nancy Williams says "What we used to have to respond to in days, we now have to respond to in hours or minutes. Cloud computing and SAS—Software as Service—has been the answer for us. In many ways it is cheaper, as we do not own the software but have total ownership of our data."

So, show that your company possesses the technology to service them in the most high-quality, efficient, and economical way. Make it easy for a company to work with you by matching your systems to their needs.

Technology Tip #2: Different companies have different requirements. Ask.

Before you panic and spend a lot of money on new technology, find out what exactly is required to do business with the corporation you are pursuing. Does the prospect corporation require that you be e-commerce. Do you need to be electronic data interface (EDI) enabled? What will it cost you? Do you have to hire new employees with new skills? How can you find out if your corporate prospects require a certain type of technology? Ask! This should be part of *your* due diligence process—not theirs.

Also remember that technology requirements can change frequently, so keep yourself up-to-date on the varying needs of your customers. Communicate with corporate contacts about their current *and* future technology requirements for suppliers. Proactive information and data gathering from the client will provide you with a competitive advantage in developing your technology infrastructure. The more you know, the better you can determine which companies you can service and the more specific and persuasive sales presentations you can make.

Corporate technology plans and requirements are often considered proprietary information and are held confidential. Therefore, it is recommended that you offer to sign a nondisclosure agreement (NDA) or other confidentiality agreement to ensure that you have access to information. Processes vary depending on the company you are pursuing, so ask about specific policies and procedures.

Billie Bryant adds that the buyer or supplier diversity executive may actually *not* be the best person to provide technological information or advice on your bid, especially if you provide a high-tech product or service. You may need to do some digging in the company to speak to more technologically involved corporate employees. As Billie points out, this additional research also helps you build even more relationships in your corporate customer's company.

Technology Tip #3: Be honest about your technological knowledge and capabilities.

When you are in discussions with a corporation, be up front about your knowledge and capabilities—or lack thereof—regarding technology. Pamela Chambers O'Rourke advises, "Whatever you tell the client you are going to do, do it. Or be honest about the fact that you cannot." It is very rare that a company will turn away a supplier who does not have a certain piece of technology, as long as the supplier is willing to acquire the technology to carry out the contract.

As with every other element of your business, never overpromise when it comes to technology. You can destroy a relationship by failing to deliver, or worse, by ruining a project because you did not use technology properly.

Technology Tip #4: Take every opportunity to improve.

Feel like your technology knowledge leaves something to be desired? Pamela Prince-Eason, WBENC president, points out that you can often educate yourself on the Internet. For instance, she says, "If you are proficient with Microsoft Word, PowerPoint, and Excel, but you have never used a flowcharting tool, you can probably learn this program in one sitting on the Internet. You can download a tutorial for almost anything these days."

In the late nineties, Billie Bryant, president of CESCO, was lucky enough to have one of her corporate customers, TXU (now Energy Future Holdings), invite her to their headquarters to view their plans to move their procurement process to an electronic data interchange (EDI) system (see more on EDI below). Billie immediately purchased the software (for which the corporation negotiated a special rate for its suppliers), knowing that it was an important investment. "Take advantage of any opportunities corporations present to their vendor base regarding electronic purchasing," Billie counsels. "Be willing to purchase the necessary software, but know that it will probably not be the last new software you have to purchase."

In fact, this same corporation gave CESCO an additional opportunity to build an online marketplace for e-commerce procurement. Even though this required additional resources from CESCO, the new technology resulted in increased revenue for the company. In addition, it gave CESCO the capabilities to perform for other large corporations. And it continues to pay off for Billie and her firm.

Where is that opportunity today? Billie says, "Now it is not TXU, it is Energy Future Holdings which belongs to a buying conglomerate called CORE Trust. Our last contract was bid as a CORE Trust opportunity. We negotiated this contract, which now allows CESCO access to the other clients who belong to Core Trust. There are over one hundred other corporations who participate in this volume purchasing group. Buying groups are becoming more prevalent in public and private entities."

Likewise, take advantage of technology workshops offered at conferences or seminars sponsored by corporations or regional certification organizations. These educational opportunities can be even more helpful than community college or adult education classes, because they are specifically targeted to MWBEs wanting to do business with corporate America.

Technology Tip #5: E-mail rules.

At the very least, every MWBE must have an Internet connection and e-mail proficiency. Since applying for certification requires the same minimum requirement, I will assume that you have this one covered and that e-mail accounts for a large portion of your daily communication. No matter how new or small your company, register a domain name, establish a website, and have your e-mail linked to this domain. You are not credible if your e-mail is mycompany@gmail.com.

Here are a few other e-mail tips:

- It is truly amazing how much business is now conducted via e-mail. Think back only a few decades, ago when most business was conducted on the local, face-to-face level. Now virtually any business can compete virtually anywhere (pun intended).
- I do think it is important to remind all MWBEs—all businesspeople, in fact—to check e-mail regularly or have someone on your staff check it for you. Do not let an important message from a corporation get lost in an overflowing e-mail in-box.

Planning

- If you delegate this task, make certain the person with responsibility has a thorough understanding of the importance of your correspondence.
- Check that your e-mail account has enough memory to handle large file attachments, such as PowerPoint presentations, graphic layouts, spreadsheets, and audio clips. It is unprofessional and poor customer service to say that a file is too large for your system to handle. Again, cloud computing is a good solution for this problem. You can also create your own YouTube channel and direct your customers to that page for your video presentations. If necessary, speak with your IT department or an IT consultant to expand your account capacity and create new technology services and products. This is crucial for those in artistic businesses such as graphic designers, writers and film/video producers, but it is generally expected of all businesses.
- Add an e-mail (and Internet usage) policy to your HR manual so employees understand their limitations.
- Make sure all your marketing materials and other important documents are e-mailable. Better yet, have digital versions that can be readily and inexpensively updated, rather than large inventories of paper brochures. Pamela Chambers O'Rourke, whose corporate customers include such large companies as AT&T, HP, Pitney Bowes, Shell, and Waste Management, says that she sends all her marketing materials and presentation materials to her customers via e-mail. "I find that the 'soft' copies I send via e-mail do not get deleted, whereas paper copies often get thrown away."
- Speaking of databases, always keep yours 100 percent up-to-date. If your company runs on a network with many users, be sure that an update entered by one of your staff members can be accessed by all users. Synchronize everything and back up everything.
- Never hit "Reply All" unless you really mean it.

Technology Tip #6: Never skimp on security.

Old economy or new economy, corporations must rely on their suppliers for business continuity under any circumstances. This means that even with "simple" technologies such as Microsoft Word documents and e-mail messages, security is of paramount concern. Pamela Prince-Eason points out the importance of security in the areas listed below. Although many of these issues appear to be common sense, they are worth mentioning when you outline your capabilities to a potential customer.

- Revision management on written documents, such as the Track Changes function on Microsoft products. This is crucial when presentations, documents, and contracts are shared back and forth from corporation to supplier. Every change must be accounted for.
- Archiving of documents. Save every draft of every document.
- Disaster recovery and disaster contingency. Do you have a backup system in place? And, if your business is primarily electronic, could you do your job manually in case of a disaster?
- Password protection. As CEO, make sure none of your employees can access your confidential files, especially if you operate on a shared network.
- Web-based storage sites for everything from family photos to legal records are becoming increasingly available and are worth investigation.

Technology Tip #7: Use third-party purchasing portals.

As you learned earlier, many companies use third-party supplier portals with which you should be familiar. There are two major categories: managed services program (MSP) or vendor management software (VMS). These systems assists a

Planning

corporation with tracking of contract and procurement data. They also provide systems for invoicing and payments.

An MSP is an outsourced engagement whereby a third-party company takes responsibility for managing an organization's contingent workforce program. MSP services typically encapsulate the following services:

- process
- management
- vendor management
- requisition management
- rate management
- risk management
- payment services

Within an MSP solution, the third party company will often provide on-site personnel to manage the organization's contingent workforce program.

Vendor management software (VMS) is a web-based, procurement software system utilized by organizations and MSPs to procure contingent workforce resources. Vendor management software solutions are accessed over the Internet and manage all procurement to payment processes for contingent workforce resources. The VMS serves as an intermediary between suppliers and the end client/MSP.

Corporate players within the MSP arena include IQN, Pontoon, Guidant, Tapfin, and Randstad Sourceright. WBE players include Janice Bryant Howroyd's Act1! and Carmen Castillo's SDI International.

Some companies use third-party supplier portals to find and transact with suppliers. Ariba is the most commonly used portal at the moment, but other providers offer comparable services. Remember, you may register on one or many third-party platforms as part of your marketing process, or you may be requested to sign up by a corporation. Regardless, these providers do offer some advantages, particularly to smaller suppliers that may not be able to afford big technology expenditures on their own. Here are some key supplier benefits to registering on a third-party supplier network, as promoted by Ariba:

- Suppliers can more efficiently do business with existing customers by reducing transaction costs and facilitating the exchange of content and transactions over the Internet.
- You only have to register once to do business with any corporation that uses a particular online supplier network.
- You can receive orders in your preferred order formats, including Commerce XML, EDI, HTML, fax, or e-mail.
- You can continue to use your current e-commerce infrastructure and still participate in a third-party network.
- Smaller suppliers without sophisticated e-commerce capabilities can use this infrastructure to do business with large corporations—publishing online catalogs and receiving orders over the Internet.
- Everything is tracked, simplifying reporting and recordkeeping. Third-party platforms route orders securely and reliably. Suppliers receive order notifications as well as transaction histories and full audit trails. All stages of the transaction process are protected and reported.

Technology Tip #8: EDI, EFT, and ERP are your friends.

Another commonly requested requirement for suppliers doing business with large corporations is electronic data interchange (EDI) software. Electronic data interchange gives suppliers the ability to exchange virtually all information with the corporation—from job specifications to purchase orders to invoices, to shipment notices to credit memos to financial projections.

The advantage of EDI is that it eliminates vast amounts of paperwork (and time), thus lowering costs for both the supplier and the corporation. If you learn that EDI is required by one of your corporate prospects, perform a cost analysis to determine if you should purchase the EDI software yourself or outsource this function. Another advantage of EDI is that it involves a standard process, so you can learn a lot simply by reading an EDI manual, which may even be provided by your corporate customer.

One component of many EDI systems is electronic funds transfer (EFT). Even if EFT is not required, Pamela Chambers O'Rourke wisely recommends that MWBEs implement it with their corporate customers. This way, your payment goes directly into your bank account, and you never have to endure the stress of being told "the check is in the mail." These days many of us pay our home bills (such as phone, electricity, and cable) online, so you should request the same of your customers. Electronic funds transfer is the fastest way to get paid—now, that is incentive to embrace this technology!

Enterprise resource planning (ERP) is a protocol suppliers may have to support to do business with a large corporation. Examples of ERP systems include SAP, Oracle, PeopleSoft, and JD Edwards. Enterprise resource planning is an integrated software solution used to manage a company's resources and business management functions, such as business planning, inventory/materials management, engineering, order processing, manufacturing, purchasing, accounting and finance, human resources, and more. Companies use ERP systems to integrate all departments within a company while simultaneously linking the corporation to its customer and suppliers. The objective of an ERP system is to help a corporation monitor and control its overall operations. As with any technology, research your corporate customers to learn if you will need to integrate with their ERP system in order to do business with them.

Technology Tip #9: Going once...going twice— many companies are going to online reverse auctions.

Reverse auctions are real-time bidding competitions among prequalified suppliers to win a customer's business. These auctions occur on the Internet using specialized software. Bidders submit progressively lower bids during the scheduled auction time. Unlike a traditional auction in which bids go higher, the winner of a reverse auction is often the company that submits the lowest bid.

While this sourcing tool has been around for less than ten years, it has already gained widespread acceptance. The clear downside to reverse auctions is the feeling that you are competing solely on price. Reverse auctions are certainly not for all suppliers, so be sure to study them carefully before participating. Many firms prequalify bidders so that they know the low-price bidder also has both the capacity to deliver and a reputation for quality and service.

If you do decide to participate in an online reverse auction, Billie Bryant of CESCO, Inc., advises you to figure out your profit margin and "just how low you can go" before even logging on. Then just be aggressive, she says. Reverse auctions are not hard; just be careful not to get excited and allow your price to drop too low.

Technology Tip #10: Outsourcing may be necessary.

WBE Avis Yates Rivers, president and CEO of Technology Concepts Group, Inc., says that her biggest challenge in servicing corporate customers is hiring and maintaining the technical talent that is necessary to supply companies with differing technological requirements. The question is, How do you know if it is a good investment to hire technical employees when you do not yet know

Planning

if you will have enough corporate business to support the resources required?

In response to this challenge, Avis suggests that MWBEs partner with a firm (or firms) that can supplement their own resources, therefore creating greater bandwidth. Or you may need to consider partnering with one or more firms that can complement your company's technological resources with different ones that they possess. Look to your certification organization or professional association for potential partners. According to Avis, you may want to consider outsourcing the following services on a temporary or permanent basis:

- payroll and benefits administration,
- network engineering,
- premises wiring (data cabling for local area networks), and
- disaster recovery/backup, in case your system crashes.

Another challenge is aligning your internal systems with different protocols dictated by various corporate customers. As Avis and others have told me, there is a cost factor that typically does not get passed on to the customer but is the cost of doing business with big companies. These costs begin to mount as you add new and different customers. What to do? Avis's solution is to outsource specific job duties to firms that specialize in those areas. This works well if a corporation requests a highly specific software application or customization that does not require a full-time staff person, but rather a one-time-only expert. Look for a temporary staffing firm that specializes in technology personnel. There are several WBENC-certified companies that fit the bill.

If you do opt for outsourcing, WBE Colleen Perrone, president of The Caler Group, Inc., points out the importance of finding someone you trust and offers a great suggestion for finding the right vendor: "When first setting up our computer intranet and Internet configurations, I met a lot of computer technicians who would charge enormous sums for operations that did not work. On about the fifth try, we found a vendor who stated that if he could not do the job right, he would charge us *zero*. With nothing to lose, we hired him on a contingency basis. He was not only successful, but has also been with us for nine years. His honesty and integrity have helped us to maintain state-of-the art technology." Who could argue with that result?

Regardless of how much technology work you outsource, it is important to train your own employees in basic technology. Billie Bryant trains all of her staff in software applications in order to provide the best customer service possible. A technologically savvy staff performs more quickly, saving everyone time and money.

Final Words on Technology

The three most important takeaways from this technology primer are to

- be honest, but unapologetic, with any corporate buyer about your technological capabilities;
- research your customer's requirements and needs; and
- actively show your willingness to adapt to a corporation's requirements.

The good news is, once you prove your ability to work within the technological requirements of one big company, it is much easier to adapt to—and win business from—others.

Now, finally, it is time to pull together all the work you have done so far—online, offline, and inside your head—to make your case to the corporate customer of your dreams. It is time to plan your pitch.

Case Study

Janet Crenshaw Smith, CEO, Ivy Planning Group, LLC

Ivy Planning Group (IVY) is a full-service management consulting and training firm. It provides strategy, change management, and leadership development.

Founded in 1990, IVY has received numerous awards and has earned a distinguished reputation with Fortune 1000 companies, large nonprofits, and government agencies. It started as a traditional strategic planning consulting firm and transitioned to a diversity niche at the request of its customers.

Today the company mission is to assist clients in realizing their success through the adoption of its vision statement as their own. Janet explains: "We understand that we must first meet them where they are and support them in a way that does not seek to judge them. Our goal is to enhance the client's understanding of the positive and critical relationship among strategy, diversity, and the bottom line. That begins by clearing up a misconception: diversity is *not* about helping those who are less qualified or "less than." In fact, diversity is more about helping businesses increase the quality of their talent pools and vendor pools. By revealing the unreasonable biases that have kept the best people out, companies begin to attract and hire the real best of the best. Our passion is balancing strategy, diversity, and the bottom line by leveraging differences in the workforce, workplace, and marketplace opportunity. Everything we do is designed to enhance our clients' ability to implement diversity."

Preparation is key to the firm's new and ongoing customer relationships. "It has been a long time since we have made traditional cold calls to develop new business. But we make a significant investment in business development. When we pitch, we go in as a team. Typically, the two founding partners or one partner and a managing director attend the meeting. We are represented by high-level people on the IVY side because we are usually meeting at the highest levels of our customers. Our contact may be a chief diversity officer, CEO, or even a board member who cares about the topic. In most cases, our first contact is a visionary who thinks strategically about the company. Our work is core business, which is often strategic as opposed to tactical."

Janet further explains with this example:

> We will hear from someone who has observed trends in their workforce, their talent pool. Perhaps they have read an article that says the majority of college graduates today are women. They then speak at a new-hire luncheon for the incoming class of talent for their company. And they notice for themselves that the demographics of their own company have changed. They return to the C-suite and observe that the demographics of that new-hire luncheon and the executive ranks are dramatically different. The question for the executive becomes "How do we keep the talent that we worked so hard to attract?"

IVY also explores generational differences, global talent, and changing norms in the workplace. "Many of our clients have made significant progress regarding diversity and inclusion in the United States, but in other countries, there are cultural differences that need to be addressed."

IVY also looks on the product side. "The company needs to ask itself 'As we reach out to diverse customers, will we need entirely different products or different 'go to market' strategies to continue to be industry leaders?' If they are already leaders, how do they stay ahead of the game?"

Janet says that much of her new business comes from someone at a company that has heard of IVY and invited them to come for a meeting. In terms of the pitch, Janet says, "Our first meeting with a client is a conversation more than a sales pitch. To prepare, we first research the senior executives in the company. We review who is on the board and who is on the senior staff. In the last few years, there has been more movement of people from one company to another. So we check to see if we 'know someone who knows someone.' Since we have been doing this work for twenty years, we have developed a lot of relationships and a good reputation. Frequently, our invitation is the result of a visionary board member that has seen me speak, read my books, or seen the results of our engagements in the industry."

Preparation for the first meeting also includes understanding the company's core business and how it might benefit from diversity and inclusion. Today this information is relatively easy to obtain. While it may seem simple, Janet says, "We look at the website. We want to know how they present themselves to the world and what they are doing. The culture of the company is very important."

During the meeting, Janet and her team try understand what the company does and what their interest area is. "Based on their industry and what we know about the firm, we have some idea of where they are on the diversity continuum. Is their interest in diversity compliance, or do they already see this as a core business opportunity? Quite often they already have a diversity program of some sort.

"Our first proposal is usually to perform an assessment or rate their year-to-date progress compared to their peers. Depending on the situation, we may ask if it is OK to interview someone in the company prior to the meeting as part of our preparation."

Her long career in the diversity arena has provided Janet with interesting perspectives:

> I am sometimes impatient that though companies have indeed made progress, they still have so far to go. I am a

1982 Harvard grad, and I recently attended my thirtieth college reunion. (Arghh!) My girlfriends and I reminisced that in the eighties we considered ourselves to be big-time feminists. We can't believe we are still talking about this subject. We still hear much of the same stuff we heard twenty years ago: "Women are not represented in the executive ranks because they drop out of the workplace to have families." This is not true. They are dropping out when they do not believe they will have an equal opportunity to excel in those companies. They are dropping out to start businesses.

If we want the C-suite to look different, we must change corporate systems and create true meritocracies. When we start to promote on real talent versus "fit," the best people will be promoted. What is "fit"? The same people have been defining fit and only now do we see that norm gradually changing.

My work includes a great deal of change management, which sometimes means making people uncomfortable. But my work also includes a great deal of bottom line benefit for my clients. They learn how to attract and retain the best talent. They learn how to find and hire the best firms. That's their reward and mine. It doesn't get any better than that!

Chapter Seven

The Second P of Supplier Diversity Success: Planning and Presenting Your PITCH

You have secured the meeting with the decision makers at a major corporation. You have assessed your pricing and technology. It is time to seal the deal. This chapter focuses on key advice for pitching to a major corporation and coaches you through the preparation of a compelling, comprehensive, content-rich presentation. Then the following chapter will sharpen the communication skills you will employ on the Big Day.

Presentation Content

Now that you are prepared to discuss the important issues of pricing and technology with your corporate prospects, get ready to combine this with the rest of the information you have gathered to this point about your customer, your competitors, your current clients, and, of course, your own business. All your hard work will result in nothing unless you can persuasively communicate it during your sales pitch.

As a successful business owner, you have no doubt designed many new-business pitches in your career, but, as you have learned already, presenting to corporate America has some unique challenges. Particularly when you are bidding against an existing supplier, you need to be sure your presentation addresses the key metrics by which you will be assessed. But fear not. As you have learned thus far in this book, there are many people in the supplier diversity community willing to lend their help to make sure your presentation is as strong as possible. Below you will find some of the best advice in the business.

Remember above all else that the way you prepare, deliver, and follow up your pitch indicates to a corporation how you will treat them as a customer in the future, so do your absolute best and never cut corners.

First, Get Personal

I highly recommend that all MWBEs develop customized materials for each corporate pitch presentation. Always create targeted media kits and PowerPoint presentations, and you may even want to design a special brochure or other professional "leave-behind" targeted to the corporation you are pitching. Make it clear that you are not recycling a pitch made to another company.

Customization does not just mean including the target company's logo on your presentation materials. It means including the company's terminology, key words, and common acronyms in your presentation or proposal. It means reading up on the company's recent activities in the news and on the Internet for several days leading up to your meeting. Show your potential new corporate partner that you have done your homework and that you have done everything you can to learn about their company.

In addition to scouring the website, read a couple of years' worth of annual reports. They are downloadable from the website and provide critical information about corporate culture and hierarchy. If it is a customer-facing company, be sure to "friend" them on Facebook and follow them on Twitter to know what their current promotions look like.

Personalizing your presentation includes the following:

- Feature the company's correct name and logo in your presentation materials. Be careful; spellings (Deutsche

Preparation

Bank), hyphenations (Bristol-Myers Squibb), and post-merger combinations can be especially tricky and can change. Be careful not to violate the corporation's guidelines on logo usage.
- Include key words or phrases from the corporation's mission statement or goals and objectives—and then tie this language to *your* company's mission and goals. Visit the company's supplier diversity website for ideas.
- Use industry buzzwords to show that you are on the cutting edge of your field. Again, comb through the website of the corporation you are pitching to make sure your terminology matches theirs, particularly when it comes to technology.

Getting personal also means getting to know the corporation's existing products and services with your five senses. This advice comes from the book *Perfecting Your Pitch* by WBE Nancy Michaels, president of GrowYourBusiness.com. According to Nancy, many smart businesspeople who pitch their products or services to a large company overlook the most obvious form of research: the "live, in-person, real-world" kind she likes to call "Research Unplugged." Here is some of her wise advice:

> If your prospect is a retail store, shop there. If your prospect is a cosmetics line, wear it. If your prospect is a production company, see their films. If your prospect is a regional bank, visit their ATMs and tellers. If your prospect makes pencils, use them whenever you write. At the very least, you should call and ask for the annual report of every company you are targeting (many annual reports are available online as well).
>
> Take notes every time you visit a location, call the company, or have any other interaction. Do not forget to enter your findings in your database. This is information that senior-level people will value when you are pitching your services for improving their current practices and increasing their competitive advantage. Make notes about your experiences

and note how your product or service can improve the lives of your potential clients...and use this in your pitch.

A Small Mistake Can Cost You Big

One supplier diversity director cautions, "Many MWBEs make the mistake of approaching our buying organization and my office with the introductory statement: 'My company is a certified small business.' It is important to understand that the only people in a corporation who understand the significance of 'small' [as defined by the Small Business Administration certification] are those dealing in government contracting. In my corporation, that includes possibly only one other person besides me. Since more companies are seeking fewer, more-significant supplier relationships, any reference to 'small' is an immediate kiss of death, because working with numerous 'small' suppliers is counter to the direction of most large corporations. If a supplier chooses to identify as a diverse supplier, stating women or minority ownership is sufficient."

Concerned about the way you are describing your MWBE status? Practice your company description with your supplier diversity contacts or a mentor in your certifying organization. As you can see, even a seemingly small word can have big consequences.

Get Specific

While all pitches are not the same and all suppliers may not be asked to address every issue imaginable, you must be prepared for any and all questions. I have surveyed many corporations to learn the factors they assess when evaluating new business pitches.

Kathy Homeyer, corporate supplier diversity manager at UPS, recommends that all MWBEs be prepared for "the $64,000 question": "If I buy your product or service, how will it help my company to gain a competitive advantage?"

Preparation

Can you answer that question for all your potential customers? What specific, measurable value do you bring to the table for this corporation? As one telecom buyer explains, "Nothing is more compelling than a supplier who says, 'I understand the challenges of your industry, and I can help you be more successful.'" Consider how much less persuasive it is to say, "We make products for call centers" than to say, "My company offers a proprietary quality check software for call centers that has proven to improve satisfaction by 30 percent."

Show you have done your homework and are prepared to deliver what the company needs.

CHEAT SHEET

What the Buyer Wants to Know

Include the following topics in your pitch to present the most comprehensive and impressive information possible:

- **Customer focus**—As mentioned throughout this book, show not only that you will treat your corporate client like gold, but also that you have done your research to fully understand the needs and goals of the company. Then, of course, demonstrate that you are a perfect match for their needs.

- **Specialization**—Exhibit your core competency in the area you are pitching. Share your experience and expertise. Be specific.

- **Cost savings and value add**—With today's

constant focus on cost cutting and streamlining, be sure to show that you are as focused on efficiency and profitability as your corporate prospect. As Energy Future Holdings Heather Herndon Wright advises, "You need to show that you can provide at least one or more of three simple, but critical, components to the supply chain: (1) cost reduction, (2) cost avoidance, or (3) increased revenues. Otherwise you will have a very hard sell."

- **Innovative business solutions**—Are you on the cutting edge in your field? Corporations want to know that their partners are continually improving their products and services. Show that you have a track record of innovation and a commitment to maintain your competitive edge. According to Laura Taylor, vice president of strategic sourcing and procurement operations at Pitney Bowes (and chair of the WBENC Board of Directors), "With the supplier diversity program, we strive to deliver on business value. Innovation has been key. We look for solutions that are innovative. Diverse companies tend to be smaller and provide flexibility in service delivery. We have been able to identify diverse suppliers that help to meet a niche need—a differentiator."

- **Technology**—You must demonstrate that you are technologically savvy and able to interact with the technology used by your corporate partner. As mentioned in the technology section of this chapter, many companies require that you are using electronic data interchange (EDI) or e-commerce for product purchases and payments. Do not wait for the company to ask about your capabilities. If you do not currently have the technological capability that you think (or know from your research) you will need, Billie Bryant advises that you show a proven track record of delivery in nontechnological ways—for example, with billing, invoicing, or purchase-order processing. Add to this your willingness to ramp up quickly, and you should impress.

- **Impressive technological capabilities**—These can help make a smaller supplier appear like a larger company. It is good marketing to show that, as a "little guy," you can deal with a company in the same way as a "big guy" can. You may have more opportunities if your technology makes you appear bigger than you are.

- **Quality processes**—Share some information about your business processes and operations management. If you are ISO 9000 certified, make certain that fact is front and center on all your marketing materials.

- **Recognition**—Demonstrate any examples of excellence in your business, such as awards and certifications, particularly from industry or MWBE organizations familiar to the corporation you are pitching.

- **References**—Share your best references to show that you have a proven track record and clients eager to vouch for you. Do not be shy about demonstrating that you have other corporate buyers. Corporations are actually pleased to know that you are already working with big partners and that you are able to provide multiple services to multiple customers.

- **Strong finances**—You must prove that you are in good financial condition. Corporations do not want to think you will go broke without their business. Although you may not offer them for close scrutiny, do take to the meeting financial statements or budgets that may be relevant to the contract you are discussing.

- **Compliance**—Depending on your industry, do not neglect to show that you fulfill such requirements as Occupational Safety and Health Administration (OSHA) product and service safety standards.

- **Readiness**—You need to be ready, willing, and able to provide the products or services you are pitching. Could you deliver right away, if necessary? Remember, never ever to promise something you cannot deliver.

Finally, Get Comfortable

Customized, thorough content is crucial, but even the best information can be ineffective if it is communicated poorly. Great content can appear just OK if it is not presented with confidence.

Practice Makes Perfect

Even if you believe you have excellent presentation skills, you must practice (and practice and practice) before you present in front of corporate buyers. Reach out to your network and employees for guidance and feedback before the big day.

First, practice your message with your existing clients. If you have developed a good relationship with a satisfied client, he or she will likely be happy to listen to the key points you plan to make with a large corporate buyer and flattered that you sought his or her advice. Satisfied clients are a good judge of what you do well and what made them contract with your company. Do not be afraid to ask for their support.

Second, practice your entire pitch in front of a "mock" corporation made up of anyone you know who has worked in the higher levels of a Fortune 500 company. Consider your staff, friends, and family, or mastermind group members. You might also invite fellow WBEs who have made pitches to the same corporation or a similar-sized company to review your presentation. Most communications experts also recommend that you videotape (or at least audiotape) your practice sessions so you can critique yourself.

Rae Waldon, PhD, executive director of the Ohio River Valley Women's Business Council works closely with Cincinnati corporate sponsor UC Health on educational and networking programs. Dennis Robb, senior vice president of business operations and chief supply chain conducts weekly meetings that provide local diverse suppliers with opportunities to learn, network, and practice their pitch. "Women and minority-owned businesses can schedule time on the agenda to

Breaking Through

present their products and services to UC Health officials and other corporations, organizations, MBEs, and WBEs in attendance. The audience at the meeting gives constructive feedback to the presenting businesses on the effectiveness of their presentation. Some MBE and WBE businesses have presented at the meeting multiple times to get feedback in order to sharpen their sales pitch." Check with your RPO to see if there are similar opportunities.

If you believe you need to get professional assistance to improve your presentation skills, take a public-speaking class at your local community college, join a group such as Toastmasters, or hire a communications coach (another opportunity to work with a fellow MWBE). Many professional associations, including WBENC, also offer classes and workshops on communication and presentation skills either at the regional level or during national conferences.

When you practice, ask your audience to evaluate your pitch on the following factors:

- **Clarity of your message**—Are you explaining your company and its value proposition or services clearly and concisely? Have you controlled the dialogue and presented what you believe is important about your product or service for this targeted corporation? Some industry jargon helps you prove your expertise, but beware of overlong, overly detailed explanations.
- **Capabilities**—Does the audience believe that you are capable of doing the specific business you propose to do with the large corporation?
- **Presentation style**—Are you projecting a confident, strong, and positive persona? Do you have any quirks or ticks that may be distracting to your listeners? Do not let anything get in the way of the message you want to convey. Watch for the following:
    o Too many uses of "um," "like," or "you know"

    - High-pitched or wavering voice
    - Too much hand movement
    - Not enough eye contact
    - Shifting from foot to foot
    - Nervous giggling or coughing
    - Speaking too quickly or too slowly
- **Presentation materials**—Are your presentation materials—PowerPoint, charts, product samples, and so on—professional, clear, and necessary? Do they match your other collateral materials and offer a consistent image of your company? See the "Cheat Sheet" in this section for more tips on creating professional presentations.
- **Typos and grammatical mistakes**—Never ever ever ever ever tolerate typos or mistakes in your presentation materials or in your speech. Tell your practice audience not to be shy about pointing out any mistakes they see, or even think they see. This issue is even more important for MWBEs pitching services such as translation, communications, human resource consulting, advertising, or any other area that involves representing the corporation through writing or speech.
- **Length**—Is your presentation too long or too short? Do you get to your main points quickly enough? Remember, no matter how long your meeting is scheduled for, you may have significantly more or less time than you think. Be aware of how long each segment of your presentation takes so you can adjust if necessary during your meeting.
- **Tone**—Are you presenting in a positive way? Are you focusing too much on negatives or challenges and not enough on positive solutions? A little humility is nice, but do not undermine your credibility by appearing pessimistic or overly self-deprecating.
- **Certification**—Have you highlighted the advantages you bring to the table as a certified business?

CHEAT SHEET

TIPS FOR A PERFECTLY PRESENTABLE PRESENTATION

Marketing and sales strategist Nancy Michaels shares the following tips on presentation visuals in her book *Perfecting Your Pitch* (Career Press, 2005):

- Create professional presentation materials. The beauty of today's technology is that it creates a level playing field for small businesses and independent salespeople. Even the "small guys" can create presentations with impressive visuals and some (but not too much!) animation. Not proficient with technology yourself? Hire an expert or even a smart high school or college student to help with your graphics.

- Do not use more than two font types in your presentation. This confuses the eye and draws attention away from your message.

- Use lighter letters on a dark background. This is more visually appealing than black letters on a plain white background.

- Avoid writing out exactly what you are planning to say—this is the biggest mistake presenters make. Never read the words exactly as they are printed on the screen. This is the surest way to put your audience to sleep. You know your stuff! Use visual images to enhance the words you are planning to say.

- Use numbers, statistics, and diagrams. Impressive numbers are often more compelling than words when it comes to a business pitch. This is crucial if you know that key financial managers will be in the room during your meeting.

- Do not outline every project you have ever done for each of your twenty clients. Instead, use testimonials to build your case.

- A single glowing sentence from each client testifying to your value (again, use numbers that show cost savings and added value) will be sufficiently impressive. And remember to include your clients' company logos with their testimonials. This is especially important if you have completed work for well-known companies in your industry—brand names really stand out in a presentation. (Be sure to obtain approval from your current or former clients before using their names in your presentation.)

- Provide meeting attendees with a printed and electronic list of references, including all contact information. Be prepared with this information *before* your prospect asks for it. This shows confidence and planning on you part. Again, confirm with your references that this is OK.

Breaking Through

I can attest that Nancy practices what she preaches. The Women's Business Enterprise National Council has contracted with her to present her Making the Pitch and Perfecting the Pitch workshops to WBEs at our national conferences as well as at matchmaker meetings around the country. I had seen Nancy present her "generic" workshop to the WBENC audience, so I was surprised and impressed when, at a presentation at a matchmaker held at the UPS headquarters in Atlanta, her presentation was subtly different. Interspersed throughout her talk were references to UPS that were current and relevant to the supplier diversity and purchasing nature of the event. It was clear she had done her homework. In addition to setting a good example for the audience, Nancy impressed the senior executives at UPS who were present.

Anticipating Questions

While you cannot anticipate every question you will receive during your meeting, some common questions are asked by corporate buyers in virtually any industry. Practice your answers to the queries below. You may want to consider including some of this information in your prepared presentation.

- Tell us a bit about the history of your company. (This is a great opening to draw attention to your certification.)
- Who are your key clients?
- Why do you want to do business with XYZ Company?
- Have you worked with other large companies?
- What are your biggest weaknesses?
- How quickly can you ramp up to integrate with our systems?
- What systems does your company use for invoicing, order confirmation, and so on?
- What is your geographical service area?
- Do you drop-ship?
- Are you willing to subcontract to one of our prime contractors?

Preparation

- Do you have a supplier diversity program in your company?
- What percentage of your spend is with diverse suppliers?
- Do you give volume discounts?
- Can you provide custom packaging?

Pitch Meeting Dos and Don'ts

- ***Don't* assume your certification will win you the business.** Never walk in with a sense of entitlement because you are a MWBE or a certified business. Your certification may have gotten you to this point, but your business acumen and value proposition will get you the rest of the way.
- ***Don't* overpromise.** This point is worth repeating. While this is a sales pitch, there is no advantage to exaggerating your capabilities. If you promise an unrealistic time frame or deliverable, you will lose the business. If you continually find that you are unprepared for the requirements corporate buyers are seeking, you may need to reassess your readiness for supplying to that market and set your sights a bit lower until you can expand or improve your capabilities.
- ***Do* show your enthusiasm and passion.** You may be small compared to the corporation you are pitching, but large companies know that one of the advantages of working with entrepreneurs is the passion and drive they bring to the table. Let your enthusiasm shine through.
- ***Don't* bring many giveaways or gadgets.** Corporate buyers will not be impressed with flashy gifts or gizmos emblazoned with your logo. On the contrary, they may think you are frivolous in your spending on such items. In fact, if they are expensive or appear to be expensive, accepting them may violate the ethics policy or code of conduct of the company.

- ***Do* take notes.** Note taking shows that you are not just interested in pitching your products or services, but that you want to be an active partner with the corporation. Notes will also remind you of key messages to include in your follow-up.
- ***Don't* interrupt.** Some presenters are so eager to give every word of their prepared and much-practiced presentation that they power through, ignoring questions, visual cues, and comments from their audience. Remember that the goal of your meeting is to win the business, not to win an Oscar.
- ***Don't* cling to an outdated value proposition.** Pamela Prince-Eason, President and CEO of WBENC, reminds MWBEs not to continue to pursue a particular type of business when the purchaser tells you it is no longer part of the corporation's strategy. All businesses experience change over time, and large growth often leads to implementation of new strategies. For example, many corporations have moved to managed service-provider structures for services such as temporary IT labor to most effectively manage these resources. If a company determines a particular structure is best for its business, a potential MWBE supplier should look for a way to work within the new strategy, instead of clinging to old value proposition. Do not pitch a product or service that no longer matches a company's business model.
- ***Don't* offer to work for free.** This tip also comes from Pam. "Purchasing officers do not like it when someone offers to do work for free. We understand that the supplier is trying to prove himself or herself, but offering work for free makes the work appear less valuable."
- ***Do* stay open to detours.** The meeting may turn in an unexpected direction. Buyers may take a strong interest in a product or service that surprises you. When their questions and interests are in an area that you can fulfill, be open to opportunities you may not have expected. Just take a deep breath and *listen* for their interests.

- ***Don't* be stingy with your materials.** Bring more than enough printouts of your presentation (so meeting attendees can take notes and follow along) and your marketing materials. Do not let anyone feel neglected, even if he or she arrives late and unannounced.

Test Your Technology

Planning to use PowerPoint, an LCD projector, a laptop, a VCR, or any other high-tech or low-tech product during your presentation? Do not leave anything to chance. Never rely on the company to provide you with *any* support, including an electrical outlet. The best plan is to arrive prepared to give your presentation in an empty room. Bring all presentation and technology needs along with you, and know how to use them. Take a minute or two at the beginning of your meeting to test your technology politely. (Even better, the company may allow you to enter the room a few minutes early to set up. It is a good idea to befriend the administrative staff and submit this request when the meeting is scheduled.)

I am always shocked and dismayed when I attend a conference and the speaker clicks on her remote…and clicks…and clicks…and nothing happens. It is inexcusable to waste precious minutes in front of a buyer fiddling with your laptop. Be 110 percent prepared, even if it means taking a lesson from your fifteen-year-old on the workings of your DVR. I cannot emphasize this point enough—it detracts from your credibility to seem like a person who cannot work your own presentation technology. If using technology is totally beyond you or makes you nervous, bring a staff person with you to handle the technology. If it's handled seamlessly, this can add to your presence as the leader and eliminates unnecessary distractions. That will leave you free to concentrate on the message, not the medium.

Breaking Through

It goes without saying how horrifying this would be if you were pitching Apple, Dell, Microsoft, IBM, AT&T, or another high-tech corporation. Of course, if you are pitching those companies, make certain that your systems are theirs and not the competitor's.

One last note: bring extra batteries and light bulbs. Murphy's Law is alive and well. If all else fails, be prepared to be calm, cool, and collected if you have to revert to a high-touch, low-tech presentation without the planned technology. Since you cannot guarantee the size of the room or whether or not your laptop will crash five minutes before your presentation, hard copies are a must for backup. Thumb drives are perfect for backing up a presentation or other material. They plug into the USB port of any computer and can fit in your pocket or purse. Materials saved to the cloud can also be easily downloaded.

I remember when a WBENC consultant, Julie White of McKinley Marketing, thought she was prepared for all events when presenting to a strategic planning session of our Board of Directors. She traveled from Washington, D.C., to San Ramon, California, for the meeting. Not only was the presentation on her computer, but it was also backed up to a CD in the event that the computer crashed. Julie had been careful to keep everything with her in her carry-on luggage, not trusting the airline with the important presentation.

After hopping off the shuttle bus at the rental car agency, she was horrified to discover that her bag was not on the bus; a look-alike was in its place. Her bag had been inadvertently taken by a traveler who, it was discovered, was en route to Brazil. The bag was recovered and the presentation saved, but Julie aged ten years in the process. With today's technology, she would have saved the presentation to the "cloud" and eliminated the stress.

If you are calm about any technology snafus, the buyer will be impressed with your confidence rather than sympathetic about a botched pitch. You can use the situation as an occasion to show your professionalism and grace under pressure. Never lose your cool.

Image Matters

In the rush to put together a presentation, fly to a different city, call your kids at bedtime, and return fifty e-mails on your smartphone, it is easy to "let slide" some elements of professionalism and poise. But now is the time to be on your best behavior. Remember that decision makers are considering a long-term relationship with you. They are paying attention to *everything* you say and do as well as the image you project.

Talk the Talk…Politely

When you are involved in a formal sales presentation, always err on the side of formality, manners, and professionalism in your language. Even if you feel you have a good rapport with the people in the room and you are excited about offering them the Best Product Ever, avoid using even mild profanity or slang. While the content of your presentation—cost, value, and so on—is of the utmost importance to your listeners, the way you speak will also be observed.

Pamela Prince-Eason tells a story from her days at Pfizer of a MWBE who arrived for a pitch meeting in Pfizer's impressive office in midtown Manhattan dressed very casually. "This business owner offered a very good price, but her overall style was too laid-back," Pam says. "While she may be able to do business in other parts of the country, she must come across in a more professional way to do business with Pfizer. When pitching to Pfizer, wear a suit. Speak professionally. Stick to the facts. Avoid colloquialisms. Different audiences may require different styles, so know the culture you are entering and respect its protocols. If you are unsure of the culture in a company you are pitching, ask your supplier diversity contact."

Clothing and Accessories

I know I sound like the schoolteacher I once was, but you must pay attention to your grooming. It is simple, but we often forget how much physical appearance matters in a presentation. Wear your best and most conservative suit (and have it dry cleaned and pressed), polish your shoes, carry a professional briefcase or tote bag, and make sure your hair and nails are neat and clean. Leave the sexy six-inch heels in the closet. If you have a pin representing your certification or an industry association, wear it. OK, end of lecture.

Be Extra Careful with Brand Names

- Do not use an Apple laptop to present to Dell.
- Do not carry an iPhone into a meeting with Microsoft.
- Do not use a Staples notepad in a meeting with Office Depot.
- Never tell an executive at Canon that you will "xerox" a document for him or her.
- And please do not FedEx a presentation to UPS.

Note that I would not mention this issue if no one had ever made these mistakes. Do not let this happen to you! One year I walked into the WBENC conference room where the staff was putting together a large mailing to our corporate members and found that both FedEx and the US Postal Service were being sent their documents via UPS. We did catch the error in time and were able to avoid offending any of our corporate members.

Before You Leave

Do not be afraid to ask for the sale. Never leave a pitch meeting without knowing your next steps.

Preparation

- Do you need to meet with someone else in the company? If so, request the correct name and contact information, and ask what the process is to get you in front of that person. Should you contact the person directly or will your supplier diversity advocate set up the meeting for you? Will he or she come with you to the meeting? If appropriate, ask for tips on what to emphasize in that next meeting. Find out how much time will be allotted to that next meeting.
- Do you need to send additional information or product samples? Clarify what is required and where and to whom it should be sent.
- Do you need to provide additional information about your company—for example, financial statements or additional references—before a decision will be made? Make certain you ask about and understand the due diligence process. If you have done your research, talked to other suppliers, and posed the right questions, you will not be surprised and should not be offended by the questions asked or the materials required. Some MWBEs have expressed offense when asked to provide financial information that they view as confidential. You should understand, however, that your financial stability is important to a company that is considering entering into a business relationship with you. Your product might be used as part of a larger process, and if you cannot deliver because you do not have the cash flow to pay workers or order materials, the company and other suppliers in the supply chain will be at risk.
- Finally, ask when you will hear back and whether you will be called or if you should follow up. Do not forget to say thank you for the time and opportunity to meet with the contact.

Breaking Through

If you have followed the above tips and provided a compelling pitch, you may be on the verge of breaking through a tremendous door to opportunity.

AFTER THE MEETING

The pitch does not end when you leave the building. Remember to send a personal thank-you note to every attendee as well as your supplier diversity contact. Most people believe that a handwritten note is the most effective. Try to include appreciation for a particular comment or action that is associated with the meeting. For example, you might write to following:

Dear Robert:

Thank you for taking time from your busy schedule to meet with me and my team on Friday. Your advice on the timing of our approach to the regional widget buyer is greatly appreciated and will help us to craft our next presentation. I look forward to hearing back from you the first of next month on next steps. In the meantime, call me personally with any questions or thoughts on things we may not have covered that will assist you in getting us that appointment.

Sincerely,

Jane Supplier

CEO, The Best Widgets on the Planet

If you have promised to follow up with additional information, product samples, references, or other materials, make certain that you follow through completely and in a timely manner. Also prepare for the likelihood that your initial sales pitch will be the first of several meetings with various decision makers in the corporation. The process of selling your products or services to a major corporation can take a long time and a large amount of follow-up and patience. Hence, the next chapter and the third P of supplier diversity: perseverance.

CASE STUDY

Cathi Coan, CEO Techway Services

When Cathi was working field services for McDonnell Douglas, she learned that companies were disposing of their obsolete equipment. Knowing that everything has an afterlife, and with the encouragement of her entrepreneur husband to use her expertise, she started Techway Services. While in the beginning the company either purchased or picked up obsolete equipment and either resold or repurposed it, they now provide a variety of services. Cathi says, "Our philosophy is simple: we work collaboratively with our clients to maximize their return on excess, decommissioned, or inactive electronic asset inventory. We care about the environment, and our cornerstone business objectives provide zero landfill *and* no-cost solutions for our customers. We consider reducing liability exposure one of our most important missions. It is our goal to maximize returns on IT assets, protect data privacy, and recover value from excess inventory with our proven revenue share and remarketing programs...and to do all this in an environmentally responsible way."

When the company was getting up and running, Cathi started calling for business opportunities—cold calling. When she called a bank in Chicago, hoping they might have some equipment she could purchase or recycle, she reached a purchasing officer who knew about supplier diversity certification and WBENC. Cathi says, "He asked if we were certified and if it was through WBENC? He gave me an education on that phone call." Before

Breaking Through

the end of the call, he had given her the WBENC website URL and told her that she should go directly there when they hung up.

According to Cathi, "That call changed everything. We started working with our local RPO, the Women's Business Council Southwest. I started calling and asking questions, and they provided helpful advice on getting the paperwork done. While I thought it seemed like a long, hard, and tedious process, they said it is 'so worth it.' I agree."

Cathi went to an event welcoming new members. She was seated at a corporate table with J. C. Penney, and Billie Bryant introduced her to Bill Alcorn and Connie Magers, who became mentors in navigating the road from certification to contracts. The speaker, WBE Deanna Becker, owner of Peak Promotions, told the crowd that certification is like real estate: "In real estate, it is all about location, location, location. In WBENC certification, it is all about involvement, involvement, involvement."

Cathi took the advice to heart, jumped right in, and asked for a committee assignment. "They really nurtured me. I was assigned to what was then the Roundup, now called businessWorks. I went to meetings, and there were corporate representatives and business owners. And everyone collaborated. I had the opportunity to rub elbows with corporations that truly care. I realized then and believe still that this is a really great organization for mentoring."

A big takeaway for Cathi was to ditch the cold calls and do her homework. "Instead of going out and saying 'Hi, this is what we do,' we now know you have to build that relationship first. I understand from meeting and being mentored by corporations and WBEs that before I make my pitch, the company needs to know I am portable and scalable and available to help them with their nationwide contracts."

Preparation

This knowledge paid off for Techway Services and their relationship with Dell. Wanting to connect with the technology giant, before she was certified, Cathi had hired a consultant, a former Dell employee, to introduce her to Dell management. In addition to making that introduction, the consultant advised her to meet with the diversity team. He introduced her to Ying McGuire, the manager of supplier diversity. "He told us that Ying would be helpful to us internally, and he was so right."

By this time, Techway was certified, and Ying liked her story and what the company did. Within two months, Techway was proving its scale and portability by conducting on-site data eradication tests in various markets for Dell. "They wanted to make certain our software product worked before taking it to market," Cathi says. "They wanted to make certain we were scalable. They gave us pilot locations to send our technicians to do data wipes."

After six months of tests and contract negotiations, Techway landed a major national contract with Dell. *WE Magazine* featured the story of the relationship in 2007, including a cover photo of Cathi and Ying and a Dell computer.

Cathi learned through the process the due diligence the corporation needed to conduct before a major contract could be put in place. During that six-month period of conversations and tests, Dell conducted an audit of her company and met with her asset recovery team. Cathi says, "At one time we had ten to fifteen projects, and that was how we proved our scalability."

The Dell/Techway relationship has grown and is expanding with global opportunities. Cathi says, "We have already performed services in Canada. We plan to open an entity there and obtain certification with WEConnect."

When Ying left Dell and Cyndi Hopkins succeeded her, Ying made the introduction:

She is our hero. She always looks for ways to help us.

Cyndi, with her team, Darlene Owens and William Irizarry, continued to carry the torch within Dell. Cyndi negotiated accelerated payment terms, which was instrumental in helping our small business. Cyndi also provided Techway with opportunities to sit on panel discussions within Dell and other events such as the Texas Conference for Women.

The Exposure for Techway that Cyndi and her team provided helped Techway to prove our service offerings in the marketplace. I am grateful to Dell for the mentorship and leadership to help achieve a successful partnership.

Chapter Eight

The Third P of Supplier Diversity Success: Perseverance

An ounce of patience is worth a pound of brains.

—Dutch proverb

A common question I hear from MWBE business owners is "How long does the entire process take, from applying for certification to obtaining a corporate contract?" The answer, of course, is that the time frame varies widely depending on your business size, your industry, which corporations you are targeting, the overall state of the economy, and good old-fashioned luck. The only guarantee is that the process is bound to take longer—sometimes a year or more—than most go-go-go entrepreneurs would like. Remember the fishing metaphor from chapter three? Well, both fishing and corporate procurement require enormous patience and the perseverance to keep casting your line.

It is my belief that most things in life that are worth having do not come easily, and corporate contracts are no exception. I promise you that MWBEs with large corporate contracts will agree that any delay they experienced in the procurement process was more than worth the ultimate reward. Good business is always worth waiting for.

Here's a personal story from my days as the first woman manufacturers' representative in the textile industry. The largest prospect in my six-state New England territory was Bradlees Department Stores, with literally hundreds of stores throughout New England and the mid-Atlantic states. I could not get an appointment to meet with the buyer to discuss my lines and why they were a fit with Bradlees's customer. My salvation was that Bradlees had what seems now to be a very progressive policy, something called "open buying days." Any sales representative for any company could show up, sign in, and wait to see the buyer. (Of course, you had to do some research ahead of time and know which buyer you wanted to see.) This could involve a wait of ten minutes or several hours, but eventually they had to meet with you.

I called on Bradlees during these open buying days once each month for eighteen months before I got my first order with the company. I tried to have something new to pitch each time and was always eager to listen to the buyer's explanation of what was currently selling in his stores. Of course, as I traveled the territory, I paid regular visits to the stores to get a feel for the changing product mix, seasonal variations, and price points. The next time around, I incorporated that knowledge into my pitch.

Over time, the buyer grew to believe that I understood his customer and was looking for the second order, not just the first. As the first woman in the industry and the only woman sales rep calling on him, I also showed that I was more than a novelty; I was around for the long haul, and my business was apparently stable if not thriving. As a matter of fact, the talk of the semiannual trade show was my new red Camaro, a certain indication that business was good.

The commission on that first sale was more money than I had earned the entire previous year. That one company had more stores than all my other clients in the territory combined. The way I looked at it, the opportunity to market to hundreds of stores in one visit was well worth the persistence. Success is frequently defined by not quitting before the "yes." My philosophy was that "no" meant "not today."

Perseverance

I carried that philosophy to my real-estate sales business. In this industry, repeat buyers are the exception rather than the rule. And when a buyer does come back, it is after a matter of years, not months or seasons. As a result, what we look for is referrals. I met my customer Mary when she was looking to rent an apartment for her daughter. Unfortunately the listing I showed her was not a fit, and she ended up with a roommate, so no deal was made.

I remembered, however, Mary's offhand comment: "With rents this high, next year I should buy her an apartment." I made certain to get her contact information and put her on the list for my monthly e-newsletter. I checked the reports each month to make certain she was opening the newsletter. Several months in, I called and reminded her that if she wanted to buy that apartment, it was time to start looking. She did buy for her daughter and has referred me to two additional clients.

THE WAITING GAME

Let us first understand why the corporate supplier diversity process can potentially take several months to several years. Here are some factors that will affect your contract:

- **Timing**—As discussed several times throughout this book, corporations only purchase certain products at specific times of the year. They may not even buy every product every year. However, they may request proposals many months before they actually plan to purchase a particular product or service. If this is the case, your supplier diversity contact or the purchasers themselves should inform you of their time frame.
- **Corporate processes**—The bureaucratic nature of large corporations means that many people are likely involved in the decision to work with you. The simple fact that one vice president is away on vacation can set your contract back by several weeks.

- **Budgets**—It is no secret that corporations have been in serious cost-cutting mode for the past several years. Large expenditures can be subject to the ups and downs of the company's balance sheet.
- **Strategic sourcing**—The corporation may already have a supplier for your product or service. Part of the purchasing decision may be as to whether you provide sufficient differentiation to move the contract to you or whether they may want to refer you to the prime as a second-tier subcontractor. The upside is that you may be pleasantly surprised to find that they want you to do more than you initially proposed.
- **Due diligence**—Many companies conduct significant due diligence on your company before entering into a relationship. As discussed earlier in this book, your ability to fulfill on a contract is critical not only to your own success, but to that of your corporate customer as well.

How will you know what your time frame may be for an answer from the company you have pitched? *Listen*. Listen for comments about the process, next steps, challenges, and time lines. Procurement professionals know that you are eager for a contract, so they usually (but not always) do their best to manage your expectations.

While there is not much you can do to speed up the decision-making process of a potential corporate customer, you can and should do everything you can to stay on the company's radar screen. Sometimes the wait may be considerable. Our research has found that the average corporate contract is recompeted only every three years. It seems an eternity, but if you are in business for the long run, you will want that contract in two or three years as much as you want it now.

If you do experience a long wait, think of ways to stay on the buyer's radar screen. This is where what you have learned in earlier chapters comes into play. Network in the areas where the buyer networks. Be certain to say hello. Send press releases and announcements of new contracts, especially those that are relevant to the particular industry. Schedule periodic meetings to discuss possible new opportunities in the company or expansion of the current contract that might provide a subcontracting opportunity. In short, do all the things you might do if the order were just around the corner. Your competitor might go out of business or just out of favor; new opportunities might arise; or a referral to another company might be in order.

It is also crucial that you not do anything that might actually *hurt* your chances at this stage of the game. Remember that the way you conduct yourself during every step of the procurement process shows the corporation how you do business. Do not bad-mouth the supplier diversity executives or purchasing officials, no matter what you think of them. Do not go over their heads and complain that you are not getting business. Do not discuss your experience with other contacts in competing companies. In other words, do not become emotional. Remember that this is business, not personal.

WHILE YOU WAIT

- Check your references before your client does. Have a third party check you out so that you neither put someone on the spot that does not feel comfortable recommending you nor get a reference that is less than you think you deserve.
- Call first and ask if you can use a person as a reference.
- Prepare a list of points that you believe are important to stress, and ask if you might e-mail it to make the referrer's job easier.
- Keep a tracking file of what you have sent, when you sent it, and whether a note, e-mail, or product sample generated a response. Be sure to track your e-mail and

phone communications as well, whether or not you received a response.
- Identify other corporations in the same industry to see if you can maximize your marketing strategy and research and market to them as well. You can never count on a corporate contract coming to fruition, so do not put all your eggs in one basket. Surely you have been pursuing several potential customers all along, so one deal will not make or break your year.

Once you have provided a potential corporate client with everything they have requested—a proposal, an in-person pitch meeting, references, product samples, and so on—your mantra should become "perseverance and patience." To revisit my earlier speed-dating metaphor, remember that the goal is not a hot date but a long-term relationship.

Perseverance

Perseverance includes keeping your supplier diversity contact in the loop at all times, even if he or she was not present at the pitch meeting. If you have any questions, contact this person first, rather than nagging the person making the decision to purchase your products or services. In most cases, your supplier diversity contact can inform you of the time line for the company's decision so you have an idea of when you can expect an answer.

Perseverance also includes a large dose of hard work. In other words, now is not the time to pray. *She* helps those who help themselves. If you are concerned about your ability to carry out a corporate contract, spend this time working on a plan for how you can deliver on your promises. Work closely with your advisers, staff, and others who will be helping you manage this large client when the deal goes through.

You should absolutely share good news and also be honest about any changes that may affect the corporation if they choose to do business with you. Honesty and forthrightness are crucial when you are building trust with this new partner.

Keep all your certifications and memberships up-to-date. Do not lose a potential contract because you have forgotten to renew your certification.

Patience means:

Do not be a pest! Calling or e-mailing your corporate contacts every day will not help your cause at all. Too much contact too often is a mistake often made by impatient MWBEs. It is better to find a balance and work on developing a relationship for future opportunities.

Maintain your relationships with other suppliers to the company and other industry leaders. Do not drop all the contacts you made while networking because you are waiting for a decision on a corporate contract.

Continue to network and show up at industry events. I got the first contract with Bradlees, referenced earlier, immediately after running into the buyer at an industry trade show. The buyer saw me talking with a senior executive from one of the companies I represented, and he was impressed by my level of access. It is never just one thing that leads to the sale, but rather an entire package.

Keep excelling in the core competencies that attracted the corporation to you in the first place. This will only help when the contract finally begins. Send those updated press releases announcing your awards and new contracts.

Rely on your mentor, association colleagues, mastermind group, or other trustworthy people to help you through the

Breaking Through

waiting period. If you do not know any other suppliers to the particular company you are waiting on, contact your local certification organization to ask for an introduction to someone who has lived through the same process. It helps to speak with someone who has walked (and waited) in your shoes.

WBEC-Great Lakes President Michelle Richards says her WBEs have great strategies for dealing with the in-between times. WBE Nipa Shah, president of Jenesys Group says,

> I stay in touch with corporate leads in a very casual yet professional manner, and now after eight years I find they reach back out to me when they have a need for a project, person, and so on. I send out casual, nonrequest e-mails wishing them well on an event or titled "just saying hello." I invite them to events that I host as my guest. I also send them out "coffee" and "let me buy you lunch" requests. Although some won't accept a free lunch, many do respond back; some come to lunch and pay for their own meal. I have established a great relationship now where if they are planning on going to events, they contact me to ask me if I'm going or not. Then they offer a ticket to see if I'd like to. I've established a great network and enjoy having corporate connections remember me without me prodding them.

Michelle adds that Lynn Drake, president of Compass Commercial, has a marketing plan to touch a corporate contact twice a quarter by sending out greeting cards and newsletters. She also builds relationships and purposely attends national and regional events to meet new corporate contacts and catch up with her current leads. Michelle and Lynn highlight the Toyota Opportunity Exchange that includes both networking and matchmaking. Lynn is proactive in asking, "What is the best way to stay in touch with you?" It has been her experience that the corporate contacts really appreciate this.

If Your Bid Is Unsuccessful

Although we all hate to admit it, sometimes patience and perseverance are not enough. All pitches simply will not be winners. What should you do if your bid is unsuccessful? The best approach, of course, is to *learn from the experience* to maximize your chances of securing a contract in the future, either with the company that turned you down or with another firm. Here are some tips for regrouping after a setback:

- **Request feedback**—Yet again, the first place to go at this point is to your supplier diversity contact inside the company. This person is already invested in your success and is likely to be more honest and helpful when it comes to discussing a rejection. Do not whine, complain, or criticize. Thank your contact for his or her help, and ask for constructive feedback that is as specific as possible so you can learn the reason why you did not win the business. Bids can be unsuccessful for a wide variety of reasons (for example, price, timing, a more qualified supplier, withdrawn funding, or personnel changes), so be sure to learn as much as you can so you can plan your next steps.
- **Analyze your timing**—As I mentioned above "no" may really mean "not now." Maintain contact with your supplier diversity contacts and department buyers to find out when new opportunities may be available.
- **Sometimes, but only sometimes** you just have to give up. You may go quite far down a particular path that does not lead anywhere. If you find yourself frustrated and your calls are not being returned, it may be time to reassess your strategy and make sure you are approaching the right companies (and the right people and departments in those companies) with the right value proposition. Hopefully your supplier diversity contacts will alert you to truly impossible situations, but you will need to make the final business decision.

Breaking Through

The good news is that, if you have carefully built strong relationships inside a company, you can keep each other abreast of changes in either of your situations that may open up a future opportunity to do business together.

When Your Bid Is Successful

If you have offered a high-quality product or service, established and nurtured meaningful relationships, and followed a targeted and persistent strategy for selling to a large corporate customer, success will eventually be yours. The phone will ring, and you will hear that magical word, *yes.* Congratulations! Securing a corporate contract has the potential to carry your business to remarkable heights and open extraordinary doors of opportunity.

Read on for final thoughts on keeping the contract you have worked so hard to secure.

SUCCESS STORY

JULIE LEVI, FOUNDER AND PRESIDENT, PROGRESSIVE PROMOTIONS, INC.

This story was told first in our second edition of *Breaking Through* and has an update for this third edition. Julie has used all the tools we have spoken of: networking, targeted marketing, applying for awards, and volunteering.

2006

WBE Julie Levi is a master of persistence. Here she shares her inspiring story of business success in her own words:

> When I first became certified five or six years ago, I got very excited and thought that every corporation in the world was going to want to do business with me and Progressive

Promotions because I was woman-owned. So I got a list of all the companies in America that wanted to do business with WBEs. I thought, *This is going to be amazing. I am going to call everyone on that list because I am certified!* Needless to say, it was a huge waste of time, and it took a while for me to figure out that this was not realistic at all.

I called Susan Bari and said, "I am just not having any success."

She asked, "What are you doing?"

I told her I was calling corporations to say they should do business with me because I am woman-owned.

Susan said, "Julie, you need to pick five to fifteen companies that meet your business strategies, which you know you can serve really, really well, and focus on those."

So I started a very strategic marketing plan and did research on companies that would be my best potential customers: I focused on travel, hospitality, finance, creative services, and consumer packaged goods. I picked companies that were geographically desirable and that fit our business strategy.

And then I started to market to them only. I learned what was important to them and what promotional products they were using. I also researched how their business was doing; if they were laying off 1,500 people, then they would not be buying promotional products.

I also started to go to WBENC conferences and began meeting supplier diversity people and procurement people who could get me the introductions to people at their companies who were in marketing or who procured promotional items. I was very focused and strategic.

Breaking Through

Sure enough, three years ago I met Lynn Boccio of Avis Rent-A-Car at a WBENC conference. I told them the Progressive Promotions story. They basically said, "You are nice, but there are a million promotional products out there, and we already have a provider."

That did not dissuade me at all. Why not? They fit my profile. They were headquartered in New Jersey [where my company is based]; they were in the travel and hospitality industry; they were receptive to WBE companies; they wanted to increase their diversity spend; and they bought a lot of promotional products. And so I kept following up with making phone calls, sending my e-newsletter, and showing them promotions I had done for other clients related to the travel industry, such as American Express and Travelodge. I shared statistics from the industry. I sent them articles of interest. We got to know each other better, and I got to know their marketing people in the same way.

Six months went by. Twelve months went by. And I kept doing the same. Eventually I got a call from an Avis marketing director. She said, "Julie, we are looking to change promotional product companies, and we would like you to come in and present your story for our team." It was a year to a year and a half of very strategic marketing before I got that phone call. You have to earn the right to present your company.

I prepared extremely carefully for that appointment with Avis. You have only one shot. When I went in I presented a very strategic solution: I asked why they were looking to change companies, why they were unsatisfied. I asked, "What is the pain in your current situation?" They said that their current way of buying promotional products was very decentralized; therefore they were not saving cost and their logo integrity was in jeopardy."

We analyzed their challenges and came up with an Avis Webstore, which provided ninety products that the salespeople could purchase online, including selected items to help them build their brand and increase referrals and sales. We included a special budget allocation feature for each buyer on the site to track purchases. Every month we provide a free reporting service so they could see exactly how much was being spent. We offered a strategic solution.

At the end of the day, Avis liked what they heard. In our first year, 2005 to 2006, we were able to streamline their process, create really efficient reporting, reduce their costs tremendously, and maintain and police their brand integrity. It was a beautiful solution.

To me, that is the beginning of the story of Progressive Promotions and Avis. We got our foot in the door. It was a nice program to start, but our goal is to penetrate our clients very deeply. With Avis, we have now moved on to their human resources department, and we are looking at international marketing. And on and on and on. Avis started as a contract of a few thousand dollars, and in 2006 it will be over $1 million. We now have an entire team working on this account—a team that figures out their challenges and works on that all day long.

2012

Where is this relationship today? At a WPEO Breakthrough Breakfast in November 2012, Avis Budget Group Business Development Manager Mary Pat O'Toole brought the story up-to-date. She explained to the audience what it takes for a supplier to stand out and named these characteristics:

Breaking Through

- Offer competitive pricing with value added services.

- Find and understand our pain points.

- Proactively relieve those pain points wherever possible.

Avis Budget Group had issues with overspending at the regional level on promotional budgets. In addition, regions were buying independently and not considering important branding standards. This problem took much time and significant monitoring. Progressive Promotions proactively created a website that monitored spending requests. It did not allow purchases that were over budget. It further ensured that all Avis Budget Group brand standards were followed. According to Mary Pat, "Progressive Promotions took initiative. They learned and understood our pain points and became one of our standout suppliers."

As you can see from Julie's story, persistence can really pay off.

CASE STUDY

TARA ABRAHAM, CHAIRMAN AND CO-CEO, ACCEL INC.

Accel is a leading contract packaging company that has built a seventeen-year track record of success based on enduring client partnerships. Beyond Accel's promise of flawless packaging, Tara has distinguished the company by staying close to her clients' needs and providing customized, innovative solutions to meet them.

Accel's list of Fortune 500 clients include health and beauty, medical and nutritional products, and consumer packaged goods—all requiring packaging that is visually stimulating, is user-friendly, and meets a fastidious level of quality and compliance.

One of Accel's longtime clients, Limited Brands, Inc., parent to renowned brands Bath & Body Works and Victoria's Secret, is a case in point of how Accel has deftly expanded its services to meet business challenges. Since its founding, Accel has progressed from long production runs to on-demand production. Now Accel can help clients respond to consumer demand while minimizing their carbon footprint.

Coincidentally, Tara was a merchant at Bath & Body Works when she first identified the market demand for Accel. She couldn't find a contract packaging company to meet her exacting standards, so she launched her own in 1995 from a tiny, 1,200-square-foot studio. As the company grew, she built an in-house team of expert engineers, designers, and production specialists.

Accel's first client was Bath & Body Works—a dream client that has grown alongside them with a commitment to innovation, superior speed to market, production capabilities, flawless quality, and unparalleled customer service. Accel leaped from 1,200 to 5,000 to 14,000 to 25,000 and then to 300,000 square feet before its most recent move in 2010 to become anchor of the New Albany Business Park East at 517,000 square feet of LEED-certified, ultra-efficient facilities.

At the same time, Tara and her leadership team grew Accel's capacity in terms of expertise and innovation. When a client asked, "Can you do this?" Accel's answer was always "Yes!"

This willingness to expand was part of the reason that The Limited tapped Accel as its first supplier to participate in its direct-shipping program. By linking The Limited's software with Accel's production line technology, they were able to ship the packages directly to retail stores in time for the holiday shopping season.

This was no small feat. Accel's task was to find a 60,000-square-foot warehouse, hire qualified staff, and purchase EDI and batch-coding equipment and have it fully functional—within sixty days. The fact that Accel accomplished this as one of many client requests sets them apart from their competitors.

Accel has also been proactive in offering its expertise to its clients as far away as China. Accel's senior managers traveled with their client's executives to demonstrate how Chinese factory workers could package goods more efficiently and with less environmental impact. For example, by nesting different-sized baskets, Accel showed how they could dramatically reduce their shipping volume and use of corrugated packing materials.

It was in the depths of a retail recession that Accel took a calculated risk and stepped up to anchor the New Albany Business Park East. Tara looked beyond the economic gloom and perceived the game-changing opportunity to reinvent the way American manufacturers bring their goods to market.

Accel would collaborate with other businesses in the Park—from bottle and cap manufacturers to fillers, blenders, and assemblers—as part of the same supply chain leading to the packaged product. The result would be unmatched speed to market and agility in meeting changing consumer demand.

In 2010, Accel broke ground on its 517,000-square-foot facility. Now boxes are automatically whisked from twenty-four shipping and receiving docks to the 100,000-square-foot "Star Wars" mezzanine. From there, components fly down spiral conveyor belts to over fifty hand-assembly production lines. Accel increased its output by 40 percent, can scale up to 1,200 production assemblers with a flexible workforce, and can deliver one million hand-assembled units per day at the peerless quality that Accel is known for.

Advanced technology enables Accel to meet its clients' regulatory requirements: it is FDA and OTC compliant. Its customized PackManager System enables Accel to track each unit within its facility or en route to deliver—an essential tool for recalling a product or accommodating changes. In 2011, Accel processed over 880 million units and could account for every piece.

Accel and its partners can turn on a dime to produce what the consumer wants to buy. If one product is selling better than anticipated in a test market, the client can change the filler and reset the packaging. This cuts down on inventory and meets consumer demand in real time.

This innovative approach and Accel's success in delivering jobs back to America—starting with four hundred, with thousands on the horizon—is why the New Albany Business Park is hailed as the "Silicon Valley of manufacturing."

Despite this strategic vision, Tara has not lost touch with the importance of shared values with her clients, such as diversity. From the beginning, Accel has honored the customs of its highly diverse employee base—with eighteen languages spoken—and drives its own supplier diversity program. It received Limited Brands' 2009 Partners in Supplier Diversity Award, the 2009 Direct Ship Excellence Award 2009, and the 2007 Championing Diversity and Supplier Excellence Award—among many.

Headquartered in central Ohio, The Limited also values Tara's personal contribution to the region. She devotes hundreds of hours annually to raising funds for regional and national causes. She raised $17 million for a regional hospice, is the co-chair of the 2014 Go Red Campaign, and is a founding member of the American Heart Association's Circle of Red.

For Tara, the client relationship may start with a match, but it thrives on a shared vision for continuing excellence and a commitment to the communities they serve.

Chapter Nine
Keeping the Contract

It is true that securing your first corporate contract can be one of the most exciting moments in your career—as well as one of the most daunting. Your first order of business is to take a deep breath and...celebrate! It is so important to take time out to pat yourself on the back when you reach a huge goal like winning a new corporate customer. Pop a bottle of champagne, schedule a long massage, throw a party for your employees, or do something else that marks the occasion. You will not have much time for leisure once the contract fulfillment begins.

Get Started on the Right Foot

Here is a checklist of actions to take upon receiving a contract offer from a large corporation:

- After you call your mother or significant other, call your lawyer, accountant, and other important business advisers. A large corporate contract can change your business enormously, so call on experts to help you make a smooth transition with your new client. See the cheat sheet below for specific advice on negotiating your contract.

Cheat Sheet

In the excitement of a big offer, it is easy to agree to terms that you may regret later. The days of doing business on a handshake are long gone. A successful business relationship depends on clear expectations and guidelines between the parties. According to Kerrie Heslin, partner with WBENC certified Nukk-Freeman & Cerra, PC, here are some crucial provisions to consider for such contracts:

Contract Law 101

- Clearly set forth the services/products to be provided.

- Identify deadlines for the provision of services/products and the consequences for failure to meet those deadlines.

- Describe the payment terms and methods, including amount of fees, billing method, due dates, interest and late charges, and expense reimbursement.

- Expressly delineate intellectual property rights of the parties for existing materials as well as materials/products that are being developed or provided under the contract.

- Provide for the protection of confidential and proprietary information, including a definition of that information and to whom such information can be disclosed.

- Identify the need for nonsolicitation provisions to protect your relationships with customers and employees.

- Consider "miscellaneous" provisions carefully, including choice of law (which state's laws apply), forum selection (where lawsuits can be brought), dispute resolution (whether you can sue or file for

> arbitration), indemnification, and assignment of rights.
>
> - Include termination provisions, setting forth when the contract can be terminated and by whom, notice provisions, and the consequences of termination.
>
> - Set forth the remedies available to the parties for breach of the contract, including injunctive relief, monetary damages, and attorneys' fees and costs.

- Show your gratitude. Do not pass Go, and do not collect two hundred dollars (or $200 million, for that matter) without pausing to thank every person who helped you win the contract. I advise writing personal thank-you notes to any and all of the people who helped you win the contract: supplier diversity contacts, other internal corporate advocates, helpful professionals from your certification organization or association, strategic partners, references, employees, and, of course, your mother. I cannot overemphasize the importance of saying thank you.
- Share your good news. Success breeds success, so make sure prospects know that you are winning business with other companies. After making certain that your new client has no objection to your sharing the good news, send a press release announcing your new business relationship to the media, existing and potential customers, associations, and your certification organization.
- This is absolutely worth repeating. *Make certain the client does not have a problem with your publicizing the*

Keeping the Contract

contract. Some companies specifically forbid this, and you must check all the clauses in your contract. Once you are cleared, regional certification organizations are a particularly great place to garner free publicity. WBENC and several RPOs, for instance, publish Done Deal reports in their newsletters and on their websites, and the WBENC website features success stories right on its home page. Remember that supplier diversity executives regularly read such newsletters and websites; this free, targeted publicity is priceless. Do not forget to add the press release to your company's website as well.
- Add your impressive new customer to any client lists you feature on your website or in your media kit.
- Educate your staff on your new customer and the specifics of the contract. Company buy-in will go a long way toward providing excellent customer service at all levels.

FAQ: What if my corporate customer is part of a merger or acquisition?

Mergers, acquisitions, takeovers, and bankruptcies are relatively common occurrences in today's business landscape. What does a supplier do when the corporation he or she is doing business with is involved in a merger? Definitely do not panic. Remember that a merger can provide entirely new possibilities for you and your business. If you learn of a merger, your first step is to communicate with your supplier diversity contacts, as always. Find out as much as you can about the planned merger and how suppliers will be affected.

If your corporate customer experiences any large shift, your first course of action should always be to communicate with your supplier diversity contact or other trusted person in the company. Do not panic. Communicate. Depending on your product or service, the changes can bring you in contact with new corporate

Breaking Through

opportunities and even new industries in which to market. Many of the diversity executives involved in the spate of telecom mergers are now in diversity jobs with major corporations in other industries.

WBE Leslie Saunders of Leslie Saunders Insurance & Marketing became concerned when Cendant (the parent company of what was then Avis Rent-A-Car) acquired Budget Rent-A-Car. "I had a training contract with Avis when Cendant acquired Budget, and there was a consolidation of suppliers and contracts. There was a time when I thought I would be eliminated from the process."

Leslie immediately made contact with her supplier diversity advocates: Lynn Boccio, vice president and Robert Bouta, senior vice president of properties and facilities. "They went to bat for me," says Leslie. "Even Bob Salerno, the CEO, went to bat for me. I worked out my contract, and now I have a relationship with both Budget and Avis, and there is room for more growth with their recent acquisition of Zip Car." Cendant is no more, but the Avis Budget Group remains a major client for Leslie's company.

In addition to awarding business to Leslie, Avis Budget has helped grow her business by providing a scholarship for her attendance at the Tuck-WBENC Executive Program, presented with the Tuck School of Business at Dartmouth.

During a merger or acquisition, a little communication goes a very long way.

Best Practices for Keeping Contracts

As you will learn, MWBEs are often quite willing to share advice with fellow corporate suppliers. Here are some tips on keeping the contracts you have worked so hard to win:

- Stay connected to all of your networks for support. Ask your new corporate customer about a formal

Keeping the Contract

mentor/protégé program. These work! Marianne Strobel of AT&T tells this success story: "One rising star in our supply chain is a WBE from our connection with WBENC. This WBE recently won business with us for a fast-growing part of our business—DAS (Distributed Antennae Solution) installations—an emerging technology where few small businesses have expertise. AT&T managers mentored this WBE and made introductions, and they eventually won a contract with our wireless organization. They were awarded a contract for our West region and with continued great performance have now expanded their business into our Southwest and Southeast regions."

- Pay close attention to your responsiveness at the beginning of a contract. Return all phone calls and e-mail messages promptly so your new customer feels very comfortable doing business with you. This is particularly important for businesses located in a different time zone from your corporate customer. Emphasize the importance of timely responses to your staff as well.
- Be willing to give up short-term successes sometimes in the interest of long-term relationships.
- Track and communicate measurable results. WBE Carmen Castillo, president of technology company Superior Design International, Inc. (SDI), shares this story of how demonstrating results to a customer can increase your own bottom line: "When asked to develop and implement automation for a Fortune 50 customer, SDI embraced the challenge. SDI's task was to bring cost savings and enhanced usability through efficiency-generating web-enabled processes. The customer's input proved invaluable in conceptualization stages, and we worked closely throughout the design and implementation of an enterprise-level web portal.

"SDI's automation produced dramatic reductions in program-based transactional errors. Prior to the web system, the program relied on manual processes that generated a historical error rate of approximately 4 percent. Within ninety days of SDI's web portal deployment, this error rate was reduced to less than 1 percent. With our technology, SDI has successfully sustained this dramatic reduction in error percentage across a high-volume, North American initiative, allowing for the expansion of performance guarantees and growth of our business profitability with the customer."

- Continue to market your products and services to additional divisions in the corporation. Rondu Vincent praises the ongoing marketing efforts of one particular WBE who has done business with Pfizer for over fifteen years. This particular WBE understands that Pfizer operates in a decentralized environment, so she markets herself to specific departments as well as cross-functional business groups within the large corporation. According to Rondu, this WBE's secret to success is that she consistently demonstrates the value and cost savings she has provided to Pfizer. She has made many contacts in the company and maintained them for years. "Now," Rondu reports, "other people within the corporation ask about partnering with her."
- Be sure to continue marketing products and services that your new customer may not yet be purchasing. As appropriate, regularly remind purchasers and supplier diversity executives of your additional capabilities.
- Keep showing up. As so many stories throughout this book have demonstrated, the business owners who network, participate in events, and maintain their relationships are the ones who consistently win business. Corporations are proud to do business with visible, successful figures in the supplier diversity community, particularly those they see at WBENC events. The more you show up, the more you are

top-of-mind when new business opportunities arise. Don't go from "who's who" to "who's that?"

CASE STUDY

NANCY WILLIAMS, CO-PRESIDENT, ASAP SOLUTIONS

Mergers have been a constant in the business world of ASAP. The company started as suppliers to Bell South in their hometown of Atlanta. Nancy says, "The rules of the game kept changing. It seems as though there were constantly different people in control and each new person had a different strategy. We had to change too." Nancy's background was in telecom, and she had an intuition that if anyone was going to merge it was SBC and BellSouth. "We had an excellent relationship with the CPO of BellSouth and asked him to introduce us to the key players at SBC." The strategy worked and their relationship with Maureen Merkle at SBC led to new business for the company. Nancy continues, "After the merger, Maureen became more powerful, and we had the relationship. When she retired and Tim Harden came in, we had to start all over. She had been president of California and became president of global procurement for both direct and indirect spend. When the merger with AT&T came about, we literally were called on a Friday by Joan Kerr, who said we needed to be in San Ramon (California), on Monday. I was at Disney World with my kids."

Naturally, they went, and the meeting was with the new president, Tim Harden. The meeting was the kickoff of him taking the time to meet with the key strategic diversity firms. Through that meeting he provided the vision of what AT&T was going to become. He told the suppliers present, "Come back to me with thoughts on how your company can fit in areas you are not currently in. Come back with options."

For ASAP "none of our suggestions panned out, but what did pan out was how we listened and came up with ideas on how to partner. Through the years, AT&T has given us many different opportunities to solve business problems and has enabled ASAP to increase our service line and increase the depth of our relationship. Business has increased 150 percent over the years through all the mergers."

Keeping the contracts and maintaining the relationships is key. "From 2000 our business has grown from $16 million to $75 million. It was slowed this year [2012] because of the failure of the T-Mobile–AT&T merger, but things are back on track and we expect next year to be unbelievable."

What is the most important factor in keeping the relationships? "Trust, trust, trust. You need to listen to the client. For example, they asked us to get TUEST certified, TL9000. When you get certified in TL9000, you are certified in ISO. It is very time consuming, but it is good from a business process prospective and it is a quality process. It is a huge differentiator for our company. It was important to our client, and we saw a value to the business—that it would also help us with other customers. We have used it in proposals. If you have a strong relationship, they will guide you in the right direction. You can choose to listen. Lean on them for mentorship and have an open dialogue. I truly believe and have found that everyone wants to help."

WBENC played a key role for Nancy and ASAP. "I remember the first Salute in Washington we attended. We did not know anyone, and the first person we met was Joan Kerr. She was the one that helped us with the meeting with Maureen Merkle. She put us in front of Maureen, but we had to show what we could do. WBENC has been the highway to key relationships that have developed into key opportunities with clients."

The End...and the Beginning

The world of supplier diversity has changed for the better since WBENC was incorporated in 1997. Cheryl Stevens, vice president of supplier diversity at Energy Future Holdings, is one of the many corporate supporters that have facilitated that change. Cheryl has been involved with WBENC since its inception, first serving as board chair of a regional partner organization and then as a board member and board chair of WBENC. Over its history, Cheryl has observed the changes in attitude that WBENC has helped to bring about:

> Corporate America has realized that in no way has the commitment to supplier diversity ever been driven by quotas or set-asides or handouts. It has been about the recognition that corporations have the opportunity to be more successful in reaching their goals, and they have a significant stakeholder out there to help them reach their goals. It has been the result of a lot of people working hard. Certification has become better understood by women business owners and corporations. From a corporate perspective, my corporation has charged me with economic development and inclusion in this space. WBENC provides me the best chance of knowing that I am doing what my company has asked me to do. Companies have realized the value of certification and of WBEs—the business reason.

Cheryl adds, "The whole consumer side has changed some, but we have a lot of work to do WBE to WBE. Women are becoming more aware of the companies that they do business with and who is doing a good job and who is not. They need to reward the companies that do a good job by doing business with them and not with those companies that are not doing a good job."

Cheryl believes that "companies understand the bottom line. CEOs want their companies to be successful. That means financial success. I have to be able to demonstrate to the executive leadership and board that I am providing a return to the company. If I am not, I add no value. The CEO of our retail company has to compete for individual and corporate business. In the RFPs we respond to, they want to know what we do with respect to inclusion. The CEO knows that he or she has successfully won business because, in part, of what we are doing with women suppliers. When it breaks the tie, this is what I cost you a year and what you got from it."

I hope that this book has inspired you to join the thousands of American entrepreneurs who have grown their businesses to extraordinary levels by becoming certified and doing business with corporate America. As you have seen, the road is not always smooth, but the rewards are abundant. Beyond financial success, most women and minority business owners say that the most rewarding aspect of being part of the supplier diversity community is the people they have met—from diversity professionals to association executives to fellow women and minority business owners across the country. I completely agree. I am proud to spend my days working with the inspiring men and women in the supplier diversity industry and the visionary leaders of diverse entrepreneurial businesses around the world—people like you.

Thank you for all that you do for your employees, your customers, your communities and your country. I salute you.

AFTERWORD

"The Top 10 Tips for Women Entrepreneurs," a 2001 advertorial Susan Bari wrote in *Time* magazine, became the foundation for the first edition of this valuable book. In WBENC's early years, at events throughout the United States, Susan found she was answering similar questions over and over. Concerned that she was not readily accessible to everyone in WBENC's growing customer base, she wanted to make the information available to women entrepreneurs and supplier diversity professionals as needed. The book sold out and was reissued two years later. That edition also sold out.

Updating the content for this third edition came at the request of the many women business entrepreneurs, regional partner organizations, and corporations that find, as Susan did, that they continue to answer similar questions. More than just a reprint, the third edition contains new content, including insightful and relevant case studies of successful women entrepreneurs whose businesses have flourished through their WBENC engagement. There is no doubt why the requests have been forthcoming. The content within is rich in knowledge related to the core of all that we do to join forces and succeed together.

Dell is pleased to support the third edition, and it fits well alongside Dell's programs for diverse suppliers. Powering the Possible is Dell's commitment to put technology and expertise to work, where it can do the most good for people and the planet. Our supplier diversity work is a prime example of this commitment; it's good for our business, our supply chain, our customers, and our communities.

We have accomplished this through a comprehensive supplier diversity strategy:

- Drive supply-base diversity.
- Enable and develop diverse suppliers.

- Expand the program's reach and relevance internally and externally.
- Launch a tier 2 program and drive the adoption by primary suppliers.
- Create the Dell Women's Entrepreneur Network.
- Launch an Entrepreneur in Residence and a Center for Entrepreneurs.
- Provide access to capital through the Dell Innovators Credit Fund.

In 2011, our Dell supplier diversity team completed a complex benchmarking project to show how our efforts stacked up with industry averages. While we still had opportunities to increase our spend in some areas, we were delighted that we often performed up to—or surpassed—these benchmarks. In 2012, we conducted a complete supply-chain analysis to understand the spending of our tier 1 suppliers, whether they had supplier diversity programs of their own, and how they were involved in NMSDC or WBENC. This yielded a unique commodity-specific foundation for a multiyear expansion of our tier 2 program.

Dell's supplier diversity team is passionate about what they do. Our work is augmented by an extended team of twenty diversity champions within procurement, who maintain their own metrics and targets, and Dell is focused on the continuous expansion of the champions. The company does both formal and informal mentoring of suppliers, and the champions regularly take part in mentoring relationships.

You have read that supplier diversity provides an extraordinary new door to opportunity. *Breaking Through* shares the insights of women entrepreneurs that have been successful at unlocking the door and taking full advantage of the opportunities that lie beyond. The information provided in the case studies bridges the knowledge gap and shortens the learning curve; leverage the content just as you would a valued mentor. When you find yourself

Afterword

at a crossroad, it might be a good time to pick this book up again. As you gain experience, the content takes on new meaning.

Breaking Through does not disappoint. I found the book to be a collection of everything you learn through your participation with WBENC. When you know how to leverage this kind of expertise, you are well on the way to achieving growth and success.

Cyndi Hopkins

Director, Global Supplier Diversity, Dell, Inc.

Appendix A

WBENC Regional Partner Organizations (RPOs)

Since 1997, WBENC and our fourteen Regional Partner Organizations (RPOs) have united corporations and government entities with thousands of highly skilled companies that meet the requirements to attain Women's Business Enterprise (WBE) certification. As of 2011, WBENC and our fourteen RPOs began providing certification for the US Small Business Administration's Women-Owned Small Business (WOSB) program, expanding the ability for WBEs to contribute to economic growth in both the public and private sector.

The success of the WBENC network is possible because we *join forces* across our network in order to *succeed together.* The certification services, opportunities, and resources provided occur throughout the network and engagement at both the national and regional level are *key* to ongoing business success. Valuable contact information for each RPO can be found below, and I encourage you to follow this author's earlier advice to "connect with your RPO as soon as you are certified" and to "engage fully in all that is provided both nationally and locally."

Appendix A – WBENC Regional Partner Organizations (RPOs)

Astra Women's Business Alliance

Diane L. McClelland, President

dimac@astrawba.org

Suzanne Lackman, Vice President and Program Manager

suzanne@astrawba.org

Lori Lackman, Certification Manager

lori@astrawba.org

5 Centerpointe Drive, Suite 400

Lake Oswego, OR 97035-8620

tel: (971) 204-0220, ext. 1

fax: (971) 204-0221 www.astrawba.org

Territory: Alaska, Northern California, Idaho, Montana, Oregon, Washington

Center for Women & Enterprise

Susan Rittscher, CEO and President

CEOCertification@cweonline.org

Jodi Baier, Program Manager

certification@cweonline.org

24 School Street, 7th floor

Boston, MA 02108

tel: (617) 532-0224

fax: (617) 536-7373

www.cweonline.org

Territory: N. Connecticut, Maine, Massachusetts, New Hampshire, Rhode Island, Vermont

Appendix A – WBENC Regional Partner Organizations (RPOs)

Greater Women's Business Council

Roz Lewis, Executive Director

rlewis@gwbc.biz

Georgia:

Sharon Judge, Certification Manager

certification@gwbc.biz

1201 Peachtree Street,

400 Colony Square, Suite 200

Atlanta, GA 30361

tel: (404) 846-3314, ext. 3, fax: (404) 745-0151

www.gwbc.biz

North and South Carolina:

Patty Mayton, Certification Manager

pmayton@gwbc.biz

525 North Tryon Street, Suite 1600

Charlotte, NC 28202

tel: (704) 444-8432, fax: (404) 745-0151

Territory: Georgia, North and South Carolina

Ohio River Valley Women's Business Council

Rea Waldon, PhD, Executive Director

rwaldon@orvwbc.org

Marjorie (Margye) Solomon, Program Director

msolomon@orvwbc.org

3458 Reading Road

Cincinnati, OH 45229

tel: (513) 487-6537

fax: (513) 559-5447

Territory: Kentucky, Ohio, West Virginia

Appendix A – WBENC Regional Partner Organizations (RPOs)

Women's Business Council Southwest

Debbie Hurst, President

dhurst@wbcsouthwest.org

Anita Steele, Certification Manager

asteele@wbcsouthwest.org

2201 N. Collins, Suite 158

Arlington, TX 76011

tel: (817) 299-0566, ext. 206

fax: (817) 299-0949

www.wbcsouthwest.org

Territory: Arkansas, New Mexico, Oklahoma, North Texas

Women's Business Development Center, Chicago

Carol Dougal, Co-President

cdougal@wbdc.org

Hedy Ratner, Co-President

hratner@wbdc.org

Debbi Lyall, Director of Certification

dlyall@wbdc.org

Deon Crayton, Program Manager

certification@wbdc.org

8 South Michigan, 4th Floor, Suite 400

Chicago, IL 60603

tel: (312) 853-3477, ext. 390

fax: (312) 853-0145

www.wbdc.org

Natasha Fedorova, MN Program Manager

nfedorova@wbdc.org

tel: (612) 259-6584

Territory: Illinois, Iowa, Kansas, Minnesota, Missouri, Nebraska, North Dakota, South Dakota, Wisconsin

Appendix A – WBENC Regional Partner Organizations (RPOs)

Women's Business Development Council of Florida

Nancy Allen, President and CEO

nancyallen@womensbusiness.info

Lisa Roblejo, Program Manager

lisaroblejo@womensbusiness.info

13155 SW 134 St., Suite 205

Miami, FL 33186

tel: (305) 971-9446

fax: (305) 971-7061

www.womensbusiness.info

Territory: Florida (with the exception of the Panhandle), Puerto Rico, US Virgin Islands

Women's Business Enterprise Alliance

April Day, President

aday@wbe-texas.org

Mariela Hernández, Certification Manager

certification@wbea-texas.org

9800 Northwest Freeway, Suite 120

Houston, TX, 77092

tel: (713) 681-9232

fax: (713) 681-9242

www.wbea-texas.org

Territory: South Texas

Appendix A – WBENC Regional Partner Organizations (RPOs)

Women's Business Enterprise Council-Great Lakes

Michelle Richards, President

mrichards@miceed.org

Michigan:

Pamela Smith, Program Manager

certification@miceed.org

2002 Hogback Road, Suite 17

Ann Arbor, MI 48105

tel: (734) 677-1400

fax: (734) 677-1465

www.miceed.org

Indiana:

Michelle House, Program Manager

mhouse@miceed.org

tel: (317) 710-0684

Territory: Indiana, Michigan

Women's Business Enterprise Council PA-DE-sNJ

Geri Swift, President

gswift@wbecouncil.org

Meaghan Kelly, Certification Coordinator

certification@wbecouncil.org

1315 Walnut Street, Suite 1116

Philadelphia, PA 19107-4711

tel: (877) 790-9232

fax: (215) 790-9231

www.wbecouncil.org

Territory: Delaware, South New Jersey, Pennsylvania

Appendix A – WBENC Regional Partner Organizations (RPOs)

Women's Business Enterprise Council South

> Blanca Robinson, President
>
> blanca@wbecsouth.org
>
> Evelyn King, Director of Certification
>
> evelyn@wbecsouth.org
>
> 2800 Veterans Memorial Blvd., Suite 180
>
> Metairie, LA 70002
>
> tel: (504) 830-0149, ext. 223
>
> fax: (504) 830-3895
>
> www.wbecsouth.org
>
> Territory: Alabama, Florida Panhandle, Louisiana, Mississippi, Tennessee

Women's Business Enterprise Council West

Pamela S. Williamson, PhD, President and CEO

Director@wbec-west.org

Maria Hicks, Program Manager

certification@wbec-west.org

1955 N. Val Vista Drive, Suite 103

Mesa, AZ 85213

tel: (480) 969-9232, ext. 4

fax: (480) 969-2717

www.wbec-west.org

Territory: Arizona, Southern California, Colorado, Hawaii, Nevada, Utah, Wyoming, and Guam

Appendix A – WBENC Regional Partner Organizations (RPOs)

Women Presidents' Educational Organization DC

Sandra Eberhard, Executive Director

sandra@womenpresidentsorg.com

Liza Avruch, Program Manager

dcadmin@womenpresidentsorg.com

1120 Connecticut Ave. NW, Suite 1000

Washington, DC 20036-3951

tel: (202) 595-2628

fax: (202) 872-5505

www.wpeo.us

Territory: District of Columbia, Maryland, Virginia

Women Presidents' Educational Organization NY

Marsha Firestone, PhD, President

marsha@womenpresidentsorg.com

Erica Kaufman, Program Manager

certification@womenpresidentsorg.com

155 E. 55th Street, Suite 4H

New York, NY 10022

tel: (212) 688-4114

fax: (212) 688-4766

www.wpeo.us

Territory: South Connecticut, North New Jersey, New York State

Appendix B
Useful Abbreviations

ASTRAWBA	Astra Women's Business Alliance
CWE	Center for Women & Enterprise
DBE	Disadvantaged Business Enterprise
The Forum	Women's Enterprise Leadership Forum
GWBC	Greater Women's Business Council
MBE	Minority Business Enterprise
NMSDC	National Minority Supplier Development Council
OHRVWBC	Ohio River Valley Women's Business Council
RPO	Regional Partner Organization
Top Corp	America's Top Corporations for Women Business Enterprises
WBCS	Women's Business Council Southwest

WBDC-Chicago	Women's Business Development Center, Chicago
WBDC-FL	Women's Business Development Council of Florida
WBE	Women Business Enterprise
WBEA	Women's Business Enterprise Alliance
WBEC-Great Lakes	Women's Business Enterprise Council Great Lakes
WBEC PA-DE-sNJ	Women's Business Enterprise Council, PA/DE/sNJ
WBEC-South	Women's Business Enterprise Council South
WBEC-West	Women's Business Enterprise Council West
WBENC	Women's Business Enterprise National Council
WPEO-DC	Women Presidents' Educational Organization DC
WPEO-NY	Women Presidents' Educational Organization NY
WPO	Women Presidents' Organization

APPENDIX C
RESOURCE GUIDE

Here are some useful websites for more information on various topics covered in *Breaking Through*. Please note that WBENC assumes no responsibility for nor does it endorse the information contained in any of the websites mentioned.

GOVERNMENT

- System for Award Management (SAM)
    - www.sam.gov
- Minority Business Development Agency (MBDA)
    - www.mbda.gov
- The Federal Marketplace
    - www.fedmarket.com
- US Small Business Administration
    - www.sba.gov
- US Department of Commerce (USDOC) Office of Small Disadvantaged Business Utilization (OSDBU)
    - www.doc.gov/osdbu/
- US Department of Transportation (USDOT)
- Office of Small Disadvantaged Business Utilization (OSDBU)
    - http://osdbuweb.dot.gov
- Women-21.gov (a partnership of the US Department of Labor and the US Small Business Administration)
    - www.Women-21.gov

M/WBE and Small-Business Publications and Websites

- American Indian Report
    - www.americanindianreport.com
- Asian Enterprise
    - www.asianenterprise.com
- Black Enterprise
    - www.blackenterprise.com
- DiversityInc
    - www.diversityinc.com
- Diversity Information Resources
    - www.diversityinforesources.com
- DiversityBusiness
    - www.diversitybusiness.com
- Enterprising Women
    - www.enterprisingwomen.com
- eVenturing
    - www.eventuring.com
- Hispanic Business
    - www.hispanicbusiness.com
- Latina Style
    - www.latinastyle.com
- MBE (Minority Business Entrepreneur)
    - www.mbemag.com
- Minority Business News USA
    - www.minoritybusinessnews.com
- Small Business Television
    - www.sbtv.com
- WE: Women's Enterprise USA
    - www.weusa.biz

APPENDIX D

EXAMPLE OF A CORPORATE "WHAT WE PURCHASE"

Website—UPS

http://www.sustainability.ups.com/Diversity/Supplier+Diversity/What+Do+We+Purchase%3F

What Do We Purchase?

To keep our business running smoothly, we must purchase a variety of products and services, which are grouped below into four categories: Services, Supplies, Equipment and Facilities.

Supplier diversity and commodity managers ensure that diverse suppliers have an opportunity to compete on an equal basis with all of UPS's suppliers. UPS maintains a global and centralized procurement process managed from the Corporate Office in Atlanta, Georgia.

Some examples

- **Services**
    - Advertising, art and audio-visual, artwork/illustration, design, packaging design, building maintenance, heating and air conditioning, building/janitorial services consulting, information services, food/vending services, graphic design, fulfillment and training.

Breaking Through

- **Facilities**
    - Architects, building design, construction or renovation, facilities management and leasing and purchasing.
- **Supplies**
    - Art/graphics supplies, boxes, fuel, promotional items and uniforms.
- **Equipment**
    - Computer equipment, furniture, airplanes, automotive parts, forklifts, trailers/tractors, ground support air vehicles, UPS package cars (trucks), conveyor and belt systems and tires.

Made in the USA
Charleston, SC
10 June 2013